BARRON'S BOOK NOTES

JOHN STEINBECK'S

The Grapes of Wrath

BY

George Ehrenhaft

SERIES EDITOR

Michael Spring
Editor, *Literary Cavalcade*
Scholastic Inc.

BARRON'S

BARRON'S EDUCATIONAL SERIES,
Woodbury, New York / London / Toronto / Sydney

ACKNOWLEDGMENTS

We would like to acknowledge the many painstaking hours of work Holly Hughes and Thomas F. Hirsch have devoted to making the *Book Notes* series a success.

All Inquiries should be addressed to:
Barron's Educational Series, Inc.
113 Crossways Park Drive
Woodbury, New York 11797

Library of Congress Catalog Card No. 84-18419

International Standard Book No. 0-8120-3413-9

Library of Congress Cataloging in Publication Data
Ehrenhaft, George.
     John Steinbeck's The grapes of wrath.

     (Barron's book notes)
     Bibliography: p. 113
     Summary: A guide to reading "The Grapes of Wrath" with a critical appreciative mind. Includes background on the author's life and times, sample tests, term paper suggestions, and a reading list.
     1. Steinbeck, John, 1902–1968. Grapes of Wrath.
[1. Steinbeck, John, 1902–1968. Grapes of Wrath.
2. American literature—History and criticism]
I. Title.
PS3537.T3234G849   1984   813'.52   84-18419
ISBN 0-8120-3413-9 (pbk.)

PRINTED IN THE UNITED STATES OF AMERICA

456   550   987654321

CONTENTS

ADVISORY BOARD

We wish to thank the following educators who helped us focus our *Book Notes* series to meet student needs and critiqued our manuscripts to provide quality materials.

Murray Bromberg, Principal
Wang High School of Queens, Holliswood, New York

Sandra Dunn, English Teacher
Hempstead High School, Hempstead, New York

Lawrence J. Epstein, Associate Professor of English
Suffolk County Community College, Selden, New York

Leonard Gardner, Lecturer, English Department
State University of New York at Stony Brook

Beverly A. Haley, Member, Advisory Committee
National Council of Teachers of English Student
Guide Series, Fort Morgan, Colorado

Elaine C. Johnson, English Teacher
Tamalpais Union High School District
Mill Valley, California

Marvin J. LaHood, Professor of English
State University of New York College at Buffalo

Robert Lecker, Associate Professor of English
McGill University, Montréal, Québec, Canada

David E. Manly, Professor of Educational Studies
State University of New York College at Geneseo

Bruce Miller, Associate Professor of Education
State University of New York at Buffalo

Frank O'Hare, Professor of English
Ohio State University, Columbus, Ohio

Faith Z. Schullstrom, Member, Executive Committee
National Council of Teachers of English
Director of Curriculum and Instruction
Guilderland Central School District, New York

Mattie C. Williams, Director, Bureau of Language Arts
Chicago Public Schools, Chicago, Illinois

HOW TO USE THIS BOOK

You have to know how to approach literature in order to get the most out of it. This *Barron's Book Notes* volume follows a plan based on methods used by some of the best students to read a work of literature.

Begin with the guide's section on the author's life and times. As you read, try to form a clear picture of the author's personality, circumstances, and motives for writing the work. This background usually will make it easier for you to hear the author's tone of voice, and follow where the author is heading.

Then go over the rest of the introductory material—such sections as those on the plot, characters, setting, themes, and style of the work. Underline, or write down in your notebook, particular things to watch for, such as contrasts between characters and repeated literary devices. At this point, you may want to develop a system of symbols to use in marking your text as you read. (Of course, you should only mark up a book you own, not one that belongs to another person or a school.) Perhaps you will want to use a different letter for each character's name, a different number for each major theme of the book, a different color for each important symbol or literary device. Be prepared to mark up the pages of your book as you read. Put your marks in the margins so you can find them again easily.

Now comes the moment you've been waiting for—the time to start reading the work of literature. You may want to put aside your *Barron's Book Notes* volume until you've read the work all the way through. Or you may want to alternate, reading the *Book Notes* analysis of each section as soon as you have finished reading the corresponding part of the original. Before you move on, reread crucial passages you don't fully understand. (Don't take this guide's analysis for granted—make up your own mind as to what the work means.)

Once you've finished the whole work of literature, you may want to review it right away, so you can firm up your ideas about what it means. You may want to leaf through the book concentrating on passages you marked in reference to one character or one theme. This is also a good time to reread the *Book Notes* introductory material, which pulls together insights on specific topics.

When it comes time to prepare for a test or to write a paper, you'll already have formed ideas about the work. You'll be able to go back through it, refreshing your memory as to the author's exact words and perspective, so that you can support your opinions with evidence drawn straight from the work. Patterns will emerge, and ideas will fall into place; your essay question or term paper will almost write itself. Give yourself a dry run with one of the sample tests in the guide. These tests present both multiple-choice and essay questions. An accompanying section gives answers to the multiple-choice questions as well as suggestions for writing the essays. If you have to select a term paper topic, you may choose one from the list of suggestions in this book. This guide also provides you with a reading list, to help you when you start research for a term paper, and a selection of provocative comments by critics, to spark your thinking before you write.

THE AUTHOR AND HIS TIMES

He didn't know it at the time, but John Steinbeck started getting ready to write *The Grapes of Wrath* when he was a small boy in California. Much of what he saw and heard while growing up found its way into the novel. On weekends his father took John and his three sisters on long drives out into the broad and beautiful valleys south of Salinas, the town where John was born in 1902. John passed vast orchards, and endless fields green with lettuce and barley. He observed the workers and the run-down shacks in which they lived. And he saw, even before he was old enough to wear long pants, that the farmhands' lives differed from his own.

Although the Steinbecks weren't wealthy (John's father ran a flour mill), they lived in a comfortable Victorian house. John grew up on three square meals a day. He never doubted that he would always have enough of life's necessities. He even got a pony for his 12th birthday. (The pony became the subject of one of Steinbeck's earliest successes, his novel *The Red Pony*.) But don't think John was pampered; his family expected him to work. He delivered newspapers and did odd jobs around town.

Family came first in the Steinbeck household. While not everyone saw eye-to-eye all the time, parents and children got along well. His father saw that John had talent and encouraged him to become a writer. His mother at first wanted John to be a banker—a real irony when you consider what Steinbeck says about banks in *The Grapes of Wrath*—but she changed her mind when John began spending hours in his room scrawling stories and writing articles for the school paper. Later in life, Steinbeck denied that his family served as a model for the Joads in *The Grapes of Wrath*. But both families understood well the meaning of family unity.

As a boy, John roamed the woods and meadows near his home and explored the caves. He swam in the creeks and water holes and became acquainted with the ways of nature. He developed a feel for the land. Each year the Salinas River flooded and then dried up, and John began to understand the cycles of seasons. He saw that weather was more than just something that might cancel a picnic. He saw that sunshine and clouds and rain and temperature readings were vital to farmers and growers. You can tell that John must have loved the out-of-doors. Otherwise, how could he have set four novels and several stories in the lush countryside where he spent his youth?

During high school (1915–19) he worked as a hand on nearby ranches. There he saw migrant workers, men without futures, breaking their backs all day for paltry wages and at night throwing away their cash in card games and barrooms. Out of this experience came the novel *Of Mice and Men*. Yet he also developed a profound respect for the inner strength of many of these laborers. They owned little, moved fast, kept few friends, and led barren lives. But they endured. In spite of adversity, they stood tall and proud. They had self-respect. Their spirits could not be broken.

In fact, Steinbeck developed so much admiration for these working "stiffs," as they called each other, that he took up their style of life. He was nineteen and had spent two unrewarding years at Stanford University. He tried to find work as a deckhand on a Pacific freighter, but ended up instead in the beet and barley fields of the Willoughby Ranch south of Salinas. Then he worked in a beet factory as a bench-chemist.

All the while, he gathered material for writing. After each day's work he wrote—mostly stories and poems. Six months later he decided to return to the classroom and to study the writer's craft seriously. Some of his pieces ended up in the college newspaper; others showed up later as sections of *The Long Valley*, *In Dubious Battle*, *The Grapes of Wrath*, and *East of Eden*.

Steinbeck's success as a writer coincided with the coming of the Great Depression. As many people around the country lost their wealth, Steinbeck prospered. He started to travel, not only because he could afford it, but because he wanted to collect material for his writing. The country was heavy with frustration. Everywhere he went he met downtrodden people with stories to be told. In 1937, driving a late-model car, he and his wife Carol traveled Route 66 from Oklahoma to California. He saw the roadside camps, used-car lots, diners, and gas stations that eventually became sites for events in *The Grapes of Wrath*. Thinking that a good story might be written about the migrants, he spent four weeks with workers in California, working with them in the fields and living in their camps.

What started as an idea for a story soon became an issue for Steinbeck. He wrote in a letter to a friend:

> I must go over to the interior valleys. There are about five thousand families starving to death over there, not just hungry but actually starving. The government is trying to feed them and get medical attention to them with the fascist groups of utilities and banks and huge growers sabotaging the thing

> all along the line and yelling for a balanced budget.
> . . . I've tied into the thing from the first and I must
> get down there and see it and see if I can't do
> something to help knock these murderers on the
> heads. . . . I'm pretty mad about it.

He wrote an angry article on the inhumane treatment of the migrants. He detailed the wretched conditions of the camps and blamed the California ranch owners for misery among the workers. Meanwhile, he had begun working on *The Grapes of Wrath*. It pointed fingers at those responsible for keeping people in poverty. It used tough language (in the 1930s four-letter words were uncommon in novels). It was meant to rouse its readers. Steinbeck chose its title from the words of "The Battle Hymn of the Republic," a song, both religious and patriotic, that stirs the emotions as few songs do. Steinbeck expected the book to be a failure. He thought, mistakenly, that many people would hate the book and would most likely hate him, too. He might be branded Communist, a label that could give him trouble for the rest of his life. His publisher urged him to soften the book, to make it more acceptable. Steinbeck refused: "I've never changed a word to fit the prejudices of a group and I never will," he wrote.

It was evidently a wise decision. *The Grapes of Wrath* is considered Steinbeck's greatest novel. It won the Pulitzer Prize and has been translated into such languages as French, German, and Japanese. Steinbeck's frank portrayal of real people excited readers everywhere. Although some libraries and school boards banned the book, it became a bestseller almost instantly and was made into an Academy Award–winning movie in 1940. The book was rarely attacked on artistic grounds, but some people called it a distortion of the truth, a piece of Communist propaganda.

They said it couldn't be true that almost every migrant was a hero and almost every Californian a villain. Almost no one denied that it was a well-written, soundly structured piece of literature.

John Steinbeck died in 1968.

THE NOVEL

The Plot

This is the story of the Joads, a family of Oklahoma sharecroppers. Unless you've spent a good deal of time in the rural South and Southwest, you've probably never met anyone like them. They are tough people, but not insensitive. They have strong feelings, and when you see all they have to endure, you end up admiring them.

At the beginning of the novel, the Joads have been thrown off their farm by the bank that owns the land. A long drought has made farming unprofitable, and so the Joads, who have occupied the land for more than a generation, cannot stay. According to handbills they've seen, good jobs are plentiful in California. When we first meet the Joads, they are about to join thousands of other poor families on an 1800-mile trek West.

Just before they leave, the second oldest son, Tom, rejoins the family after having spent four years in prison. He brings with him a former preacher, Jim Casy, who has recently given up his worship of a divine God and now believes that the holy spirit can be found in people's love for one another. Casy's idea becomes a major theme in the novel.

The Joads buy a used truck and pile it high with their belongings. At the last minute, however, Grampa Joad refuses to go. He cannot tear himself away from the land of his roots. Knowing that they must stick together, the family numbs the old man with medicine and loads him onto the truck. But not long after, Grampa dies and is buried alongside Route 66, the main road west. While crossing the desert on the last leg of the journey to California, Granma dies too.

Between the chapters that tell the story of the Joad family, we find so-called intercalary, or interchapters. Usually odd-numbered, these interchapters tell the story of the Dust Bowl and the migrant workers' life on the road. Taken all together, the interchapters show us the social and historical background of events in the story. They also are Steinbeck's way of expressing his opinions about some of America's social ills in the 1930s. His viewpoint is crystal clear: Steinbeck sympathizes with the migrants and condemns the banks, the police, the landowners, and anyone else who contributes to the migrants' plight. But he also believes that, in spite of maltreatment, the poor and dispossessed workers have a nobility and inner strength that will assure their survival. He advocates the need for workers to band together: in their unity they will find the power to claim their rightful place in American society.

Once in California, the Joads discover the truth of the rumors they heard en route: as migrants they are not welcome; there are too few jobs. When they can find work, the pay is so low that they can barely afford food. They are forced to settle in squalid camps called Hoovervilles. In one camp Tom Joad gets into a fight with an abusive deputy. When the sheriff comes to arrest Tom, Casy offers to go to jail in his place.

After a time they find a government-run camp where life is fairly decent, but they can't find jobs nearby. So they move to a peach-growing area where pickers are needed. As they drive into the Hooper Ranch to claim jobs, they notice an angry crowd at the gate. That night Tom discovers that the crowd is a group of workers on strike and that Casy is the strike leader. Casy convinces Tom that all the working people must stick together.

A band of thugs hired by the ranch owners kills Casy. In the melee, Tom strikes and kills one of Casy's murderers. But Tom's face is gashed. To keep Tom from being caught, the family conceals him between mattresses on their truck, and flees the Hooper Ranch. Next, the Joads settle in a camp made up of abandoned railroad boxcars. Tom's little sister Ruthie brags in public about her fugitive brother, forcing Tom to hide in a cave. Finally, he decides to go off on his own and carry on Casy's work.

The Joads find work picking cotton, but huge rains cause floods. The family has no food and little hope. The oldest daughter, Rose of Sharon, gives birth to a stillborn child. As the book ends, Rose of Sharon, realizing that people need each other to survive, breast-feeds a dying stranger.

The Characters

The Joad Family

Although each person in the Joad family is a separate individual, the family often acts as though it were one person. It makes decisions as a group, travels as a single unit, and reacts uniformly to events. Yet the family's personality is derived from the distinct qualities of each member. Uncle John is sad and lonely; Granma is religious; Al loves a good time. And Ma, the sturdy one, is the centerpiece of the Joads, around whom the whole family gathers. If you examine all the Joads—Grampa, Pa, Tom, Noah, Rose of Sharon,

Ruthie, and Winfield—each can be tagged with a different label. Even Connie, who is a Joad only by marriage, contributes to the complex personality of the family.

As you might expect, experience changes the family's personality. Who wouldn't change after being evicted from home, traveling half-way across the continent, and scrounging for bread? Before the Joads leave home, Granma and Grampa rule the roost, at least in name. When the family breaks its ties to the land and joins the migrant exodus, the old generation gives way to the new. Pa becomes the leader, but his authority is fleeting. Ma gradually takes over. Her powerful personality and steady hand hold the family together for a time, in spite of forces that threaten to tear it apart. When, for example, Tom plans to remain with the Wilsons' disabled car until it's fixed, Ma vows to smash him with a jack handle if he insists that the family go on without him. The rest of the family is amazed at Ma's forcefulness, but from then on she is the leader of the Joads.

She oversees an increasingly fragmented group of people. Grampa and Granma die; Noah and Connie go their own ways; Al takes up with his fiancée's family; and Tom finally leaves in order to carry Casy's message to the workers.

It's literally true that Ma fails to hold the family together. Does that mean that she is a failure? You could take that position, but you also have to take into account that Ma eventually adopts a much larger family—the family of Man—to replace the one she's lost.

Presumably the Joads' experience parallels that of countless migrant families. Should we assume, therefore, that Steinbeck intends to show us how a whole class of good and honest migrant farmers wilted under social and economic pressure? That may be so if you think that the Joads' breakup represents their failure as a family. On the other hand, since many of the Joads remain undefeated in the end, Steinbeck may want us to admire the migrants' ability to endure, even against insurmountable odds.

At the end of the book the Joads have lost their family identity. But they've replaced it with something equally worthy: they've found kinship with other migrant families. The Joads merge with the Wainwrights, and earlier in the book, with the Wilsons, because each family needed the other. When "I," as Steinbeck writes, becomes "we," the fragmented family becomes whole again. The members don't share last names, but they give sustenance and support to each other in the form of food, blankets, a kind word, medicine, advice, even love. At the book's end, Rose of Sharon shares the milk from her breast with a dying man she has never seen before. That the man is a human being in need is reason enough to treat him like family.

When isolated families fuse with one another, a larger family, a family of Man, develops. Numerous characters and events in *The Grapes of Wrath* help transform the Joads into members of a universal family. Think of what Casy says about the soul—that nobody has an individual soul, but everybody's just got a piece of a great big soul. By opening their tent to the Joads, the Wilsons are saying, "Welcome, brother!" At the Weedpatch Camp, the Wallaces, father and son, invite Tom Joad to work alongside them, even though they'll earn less money as a result. Casy lives and dies for others, and at the end Tom will walk in Casy's footsteps. Finally, when Rose of Sharon offers her milk to a stranger, she wears an enigmatic smile, suggesting that she, too, has discovered the joy that comes from adopting all men as brothers.

Tom Joad

Imagine what *The Grapes of Wrath* would be like if Steinbeck had made Tom Joad a tractor repairman or dry-goods merchant instead of an ex-convict. If Tom were meek and mild, someone like Rose of Sharon's husband Connie, for instance, what would be lost? Think of what Tom can do that Connie wouldn't dare. We know that Tom, who killed a man in a drunken brawl, can burst into violence at any moment, especially when provoked. Tom almost instinctively knocks the abusive deputy sheriff off his feet during a scuffle at the Hooverville camp, for example. Later, in a rage, he clubs to death the man who kills Casy. As one of the principal characters in the story, Tom has to be someone sturdy enough not just to take care of himself but to support and defend others.

There's no doubt that Tom has a quick temper. He speaks harshly to the truck driver who gives him a lift; he scolds the one-eyed man for feeling self-pity; he tells off the fat man who runs the filling station. Perhaps Tom's belligerence can be explained by his four years in prison, although he claims to have no regrets about them. However, there may be another explanation. If you ignore what he says and ask why he berates these people, you find that Tom doesn't despise each man, but only what each stands for. Each feels defeated by life's hardships. Tom gives them all a brutally frank pep talk, as though he wants to get them moving again. Tom can't just throw up his hands and walk away from problems. And he doesn't want to see others do that either.

Tom is on parole. If he gets in trouble or is caught leaving Oklahoma, he could be sent right back to McAlester. You might expect that a man in constant danger of being imprisoned would be less aggressive, but sitting back is not in Tom's nature. If it were, we'd never have seen him going off at the end of the book to devote his life to help organize strikes.

Just as Tom accepted his prison sentence, he accepts the harsh blows that Nature and the banks have dealt to his family. What he cannot tolerate, however, is unfair or abusive treatment. He hates being forced to hide from the deputies on his very own land, for example. Several times in the novel Tom and others get pushed around by the authorities. What makes Tom strike out at abuses? Is it his strong sense of fairness? Or is Tom merely a victim of a short temper? Perhaps both impulses rule Tom to some extent.

Although Tom is not easy to like, you'd probably want him on your side in a tough situation. He is loyal, straightforward, and realistic, especially at the start of the novel. In contrast to Casy, who is a visionary, Tom has both feet planted on the dusty ground. He is concerned only about the here and now— where the next meal will come from, where to stay that night, how to keep the car running. He has no time for sentimentality. When his brother Al wants to tell him about Ma's feelings toward him, Tom replies, "S'pose we talk 'bout some other stuff."

Tom's inability to deal with feelings does not make him a callous person. He has strong affection for Casy, for Ma, and for Pa, too. In fact, he admires everyone who struggles to make an honest living without stepping on others. He can't abide people who throw their weight around, such as the proprietor of the Hooverville camp, the sheriffs and their deputies, and the guards at Hooper Ranch. Without Ma's firm hand on him, Tom would probably have attacked some of these authoritarians, and who can blame him?

As the Joads wander around California, Tom meets more good people who keep up the increasingly difficult struggle to live a decent life. He admires their strength, and he can't stand by idly when they are mistreated. To save Floyd from unjust arrest, Tom knocks down the deputy. To keep peace at the Saturday night dance, Tom stands watch. And to find out why workers at the Hooper Ranch entrance were angry, he ignores the guards' order to mind his own business. In the darkness he slides under the barbed wire fence surrounding the compound, meets Casy, and learns the true story of the strike.

From then on, Tom follows in Casy's footsteps. His concerns extend beyond himself and his family. They now include all downtrodden people. He feels a calling to help in any way he can. Casy's violent death probably hastens Tom's decision to work for the welfare of all poor people. While hiding from the police, Tom has a chance to think. He thinks about the meaning of Casy's words—that a man is no good alone, and that a "fella ain't got a soul of his own, but on'y a piece of a big one. . . . " Tom becomes Casy's heir and disciple. If you think of Casy as a Christ-like figure, a good man with a message of love for the world, then Tom is like St. Paul—a tough, realistic organizer who will try to spread the word and make Casy's idealism a reality. As he says to Ma just before he leaves the family forever, "I'll be aroun' in the dark, I'll be

ever'where—wherever you look. Wherever they's a
fight so hungry people can eat, I'll be there. Wherever
they's a cop beatin' up a guy, I'll be there." Tom may
end up dead, like Casy, but is there any doubt he'll go
down swinging?

Ma Joad

Ma Joad holds the fate of her family in her big, thick
hands. Without her the family ceases to function: Pa
doesn't make decisions; Uncle John wallows in self-
reproach; Rose of Sharon falls prey to superstition and
doubt; Al goes off chasing girls; and the two young
children, Ruthie and Winfield, grow up without discipline. Had Ma not stood her ground and threatened
him with a jack handle, even Tom would have abandoned his kinfolk sooner than he did.

By the end of the novel we know Ma better than
any other Joad, for we see her in more different situ-
ations than anyone else. Yet she is not considered the
main character—although you probably could make a
case for it. We see Ma first when she greets Tom, just
back from prison. The family, curious about prison
life, views Tom as some sort of hero. But not Ma.
She's interested in Tom's frame of mind. "They didn'
do nothin' in that jail to rot you out with crazy mad?"
she asks. Ma's interest in the inner person sets her
apart from the others in the family. She searches for
meaning in people and events. When Casy tells the
Joads about his religious conversion in the hills, Ma
studies him, her eyes "questioning, probing and
understanding."

Ma derives meaning in life from her family. She
needs to protect them, guide them, help them feel
safe. It's clear why Steinbeck calls her the citadel of the
family. Most of all, she provides the family with nour-
ishment—physical as well as moral. In scene after

scene we see Ma buying groceries, preparing meals, doling out victuals. Even when food is scarce, she manages to scrape meals together, and sometimes she feeds strangers, too. With Ma around, no one ever goes hungry.

She has a harder time providing moral support. She would like everyone in her family to live decently, but life on the road and in the camps won't allow it. The best she can do is set an example and hope that others will be buoyed by her courage and optimism. In some ways she seems almost too good to be true. How sturdy she seems when she burns all her letters on the night before the family takes to the road. To keep the family moving, she cradles Granma's body in her arms all through the night of the desert crossing, after which Casy observes, ". . . there's a woman so great with love—she scares me. Makes me afraid an' mean." She comforts Rose of Sharon repeatedly and serves as peacekeeper when Al and Connie exchange harsh words. Only to Tom does she express doubts about the future, that maybe California "ain't so nice."

Ma's main ambition is to keep the family intact. Each time a person dies or leaves, Ma suffers a personal defeat. Even though the Joads leave home with 13 people and are left at the end with only six, you never get the feeling that Ma has failed. She's done her best, which in itself is a type of triumph. Also, her determination to go on strengthens with each harsh turn of events. In flight from the burning squatters' camp, she hails the promise of the people: "Us people will go on livin'. . . . They ain't gonna wipe us out. Why, we're the people—we go on."

As her immediate family dissolves, Ma adopts a larger group, the people, as her family. Don't Casy's words about Ma's boundless love seem prophetic now? "Use' ta be the fambly was fust," Ma tells Mrs. Wainwright in the boxcar. "It ain't so now. It's anybody." Realistically, Ma can't include everybody in her concept of family. She must be talking about people in need—the poor, homeless, downtrodden rejects of society.

Ma is not a leader of the people, as Casy tries to be and Tom may one day become. Rather, she embodies the qualities of the people. Since Steinbeck often uses characters as symbols, you might think of Ma as symbolic of the people's strength and endurance. But you can recognize human qualities in Ma as well. She's sentimental, loving, protective, and feisty.

As the novel ends, the flood waters rise and the food runs out. Conditions for the migrants could not be worse. By all rights, they should finally be crushed. But they're not. The migrant families will endure regardless of any hardship they meet, for when defeat is near they can depend on dauntless figures like Ma Joad to carry them through.

Jim Casy

Do you find it surprising that Jim Casy, one of the three most important characters in *The Grapes of Wrath*—along with Tom and Ma Joad—does not appear in about one-third of the book? He disappears from the time of his arrest until Tom meets him again outside Hooper Ranch. Yet we rarely forget him; the Joad family reminds us of him repeatedly. Both Ma and Tom often recall Casy's ideas and words.

Casy carries weight because of what he says rather than what he does. He talks a lot. As a former preacher, he is used to talking, and although he's given up his trade, he can't keep still. What has changed, however, is what he talks about.

We hear him tell Tom about his recent retreat from organized Christian religion. Hypocrisy and a weakness for women have forced him to reexamine his beliefs. After some hard thinking it came to him that sex was no sin, just something that people do. He also discovered that he didn't need Jesus and God to explain the love he felt for life and people. People, in fact, were what he loved most—much more than Jesus, who was just someone about whom stories were told. As for the individual soul, which each person is supposed to tend all his life, well, that didn't make sense to Casy any more. "Maybe all men got one big soul ever'body's a part of," he says to Tom soon after the two men meet.

Casy describes his avid love for people as a force so strong it makes him "fit to bust." Despite his enthusiasm, though, he's in a dilemma. He's got something to give and no one to give it to. Most of the people have abandoned their farms and are moving away. All except Muley Graves, whose solitary rebellion triggers a thought in Casy's mind. Muley innocently mumbles an idea about sharing a jack rabbit with Casy and Tom for dinner. "I ain't got no choice in the matter," he says. If another fellow is hungry, he can't just go away and eat alone. "Muley's got a-holt of somepin," responds Casy, "an' it's too big for him, an' it's too big for me." What Muley had "a-holt" of was a philosophy of life, a credo to live by. That night, instead of sleeping, Casy figures out how he can act on Muley's idea. When you consider Casy's actions in the remainder of the book, you can probably infer what thoughts churned in his mind that night.

Casy can't act on his principles right away. First he must find the means to get to California. Fortunately, Ma Joad, always the generous soul, invites Casy to join her family. En route, he earns his keep. Even though he's no longer a man of God, he says grace, performs funeral rites for Grampa, and helps Tom repair the Wilsons' car.

In Hooverville, Casy at last gets his chance to practice what he has started to preach. Tom trips the deputy sheriff who wants to arrest Floyd, an innocent man. Casy joins the fray and knocks the man out with a kick to the neck. When the sheriff returns to haul Tom to jail, Casy volunteers to go in Tom's place: "Somebody got to take the blame . . . an' I ain't doin' nothin' but set aroun'." You could argue that someone who espouses love, as Casy does, has no business kicking fallen men, but Casy's action may be justified in this case because the deputy was aiming his rifle at Floyd, fleeing into the willows.

Months later we run into Casy again. Out of jail, he has begun to organize the workers, and in fact, he leads the strike at Hooper Ranch. He has translated his love for people into an effort to show them that their strength lies in collective action. Love can help them only so much. But if the love he feels can be turned into work in their behalf, then his love will serve some useful purpose. He tells the people that together they have power; fragmented, they don't stand a chance against their oppressors.

Because union organizers are less popular than frost among the fruit farmers, Casy has undertaken a perilous occupation. The owners won't stand for unionization and will resort to strong-arm tactics to prevent it. In spite of the risk, Casy devotes his life—and ultimately gives it—to the union movement.

On the night of Tom and Casy's reunion, thugs come to find Casy. As he is about to be clubbed to death, Casy turns to his attackers and says, "You fellas don' know what you're doin'." In effect, Casy sacrifices himself so that others may be better off. His action is Christ-like, and his final words call to mind Christ's last words, too. Perhaps it is more than a coincidence that Casy's initials are J.C.

Pa Joad

If *The Grapes of Wrath* were a typical American novel about Oklahoma sharecroppers, you might reasonably expect the father to be strong and virile. But the novel isn't typical and Pa Joad doesn't fit the mold.

By tradition, age, and sex, Pa is the head of the Joad family. (Don't count Grampa Joad because he's gone silly in the head.) When the family holds meetings to make decisions, Pa presides. Pa convinces the family to bury Grampa in a roadside grave, and Pa rallies the men at the boxcar camp to help build a floodwall. Nevertheless, Pa often takes a back seat to Ma as head of the family. Steinbeck tells us that Pa "could not know hurt or fear unless she [Ma] acknowledged hurt or fear." A man who depends on another to confirm his own feelings has got to be rather wobbly.

Before the Joads become migrants, Pa probably couldn't admit, either to himself or others, that Ma was made of sturdier stuff than he. It would hurt too much. Once on the road, however, the old ways don't count anymore. Ma's revolt—when she vows to clobber with a jack handle anyone who dares to defy her word—puts Pa firmly in second place. Never again can he even pretend to be the leader, at least not within the family.

If Ma is solid oak, Pa is soft wood—pliable and easily split. On the night that Noah, the first-born son, came into the world, for example, Pa cracked. Alone in the house with Ma, the poor woman shrieking in agony, Pa panicked. He tried to pull the baby from the womb, twisting and stretching the head in the process. Noah grew up strange, always slightly out of touch with the world. Whenever Pa saw Noah, he felt ashamed.

It made sense for Steinbeck to give Ma Joad a faltering husband. Throughout the novel Ma has enough to contend with; she doesn't need a scrappy mate, too. In fact, Ma's perseverance stands out in contrast to Pa's infirmities. When Pa sags, Ma bolsters him. Pa tells her that going out daily to look for work and coming back empty-handed "puts a weight on ya." Ma deliberately tries to anger him to test his grit. She claims that men who don't do their jobs don't have the right to make decisions. If Pa were a broken man, he wouldn't respond to her taunts. But he comes back at her in a rage, and Ma is so pleased. It shouldn't surprise us. Why shouldn't Pa stay whole with Ma around to hold him together?

Uncle John

Uncle John divides his life into two parts: there's the part before his wife died and the part after. We don't hear much about the earlier years. But we know that John has been in pain every day since his tragic loss.

In time, most people recover from the loss of loved ones. Why hasn't John? We overhear Tom Joad telling Casy why: "He figures it's his fault his woman died." John feels guilty for refusing to call the doctor when his young bride of four months complained of stomach pains. He gave her a dose of painkiller instead. The next day she died of a burst appendix.

John considers his misdeed a sin, for which he has to suffer every day of his life. Sometimes he can't take the torment and drowns his woes in drink.

He blames the Joad family's misfortunes on himself and his sin. He also calls himself a burden on the family. Maybe, he says, he should have stayed back in

Oklahoma. Is John belittling himself to win sympathy? Perhaps, because people who tear themselves down are often asking indirectly for a shoulder to lean on. If all he wants is a word of encouragement, though, he's picked the wrong group. The Joads are pretty tired of John's whining and often tell him to keep still and pull himself together.

If John weren't a Joad, he'd be like one of the roadside characters that the family meets—a man like the fat filling-station attendant and the one-eyed man in the junk yard. He'd need a good talking-to by Tom Joad, who'd tell him to quit wallowing in self-pity and start making something of himself. But since he is a Joad, Pa's older brother, in fact, the family carries him along.

Does John seem out of place in a family that symbolizes endurance and courage? Perhaps, but the Joads accommodate him easily. Then, too, John's weaknesses contrast with the others' strengths. Having a member of the clan who's mired in melancholy—and what family doesn't have one?—helps make the Joads altogether more human.

Near the end of the story, Uncle John surprises us. He volunteers to bury Rose of Sharon's stillborn baby. But instead of finding a burial site, he launches the apple-crate coffin into a roadside stream and shouts, "Go down an' tell 'em. Go down in the street and rot an' tell 'em that way." In his own way John has reenacted the moment in the Old Testament when Moses' mother sends her infant son into the bulrushes to keep him from growing up in bondage. In his version of the incident, John sends a bitter message to the world about the conditions of his people. It's his most daring act in the whole novel.

Al Joad

During the story, Al Joad, the third son (after Noah and Tom), leaps from youth to adulthood. We meet him first when he's returning from a night of "tom-cattin'," or girl-chasing. That's what he does with his life—he enjoys himself. In some ways he's a little kid. He admires his big brother Tom, for example, not for Tom's meritorious qualities but for his reputation as a killer. Tom's parole disappoints Al. He would have preferred Tom to break out of prison.

Al represents a new breed of Joads. He plans to leave the land. Someday Al wants to own a garage in town because he knows a lot about cars and engines.

When the family takes to the road, Al's knowledge becomes very important. He's assigned the task of buying a truck and keeping it in good repair. It's a big responsibility, which he takes very seriously.

Because Al has suddenly become a vital member of the family, he is taken into the circle of adult men who make decisions. Underneath, however, Al is still a boy. He lacks the confidence of manhood. Every time the truck breaks down he's afraid that he'll be blamed. He doesn't want to disappoint the family, especially not Tom. After the Wilsons' Dodge breaks a con-rod (short for "connecting rod," a rigid rod that transmits power from the crankshaft to a piston in an internal combustion engine), Ma rescues him from self-doubt. She tells Al, "It ain't your fault."

Tom, on the other hand, pushes his kid brother. He won't allow Al to feel sorry for himself. If Al is going to be a man, he'll have to act and feel like one. When Al makes up an excuse for a burned-out bearing even though no one has blamed him, Tom lashes out:

"Young fella, all full a piss an' vinegar. Wanta be a hell of a guy all the time. But, goddamn it, Al, don' keep ya guard up when nobody ain't sparrin' with ya. You gonna be all right."

Although he continues to leave broken-hearted girls behind him as the family wanders around California, Al does turn out all right at the end. He's the last Joad to leave the family. When flood waters damage the truck almost beyond repair, he knows his job as family mechanic is done. Guiltlessly, he can set off on his own, shape a life as a garage owner. His love life has settled down, too, for he plans to marry Aggie Wainwright.

Rose of Sharon

They say that mothers-to-be are sometimes irritable, often sickly, and always unpredictable. Rose of Sharon, the Joads' older daughter, qualifies in all three respects.

Anyone on a difficult overland journey has every right to become upset and cross. But because she's pregnant, Rose of Sharon complains more than most, particularly after the family reaches California.

She frets mostly over her baby. Will it be healthy if she can't get good food to eat? Will the baby be hurt by a bumpy road? The family dog gets killed on the highway as Rose of Sharon looks on. Will the shock harm the infant?

A religious fanatic at the government camp plants the thought in Rose of Sharon's head that sinful mothers make their babies die. Rose of Sharon thinks she's sinned by dancing and by acting in a play back in Oklahoma. In spite of Ma's assurances, Rose of Sharon can't stop believing that if her baby isn't damned in one way, it is doomed in another.

Do Rose of Sharon's antics make her seem immature, almost too young to be a mother? She is at a tender age, probably not yet 18. When Tom left for prison four years back, she was only a child. Now she's a woman, married to Connie Rivers.

Connie and Rose of Sharon set themselves apart from the mundane matters that occupy the rest of the family. They focus solely on the baby. That they are bringing new life to the world allows them to dwell in the future instead of the here and now. They dream of the house they'll buy for the baby in California, about the car they'll drive, and about Connie's schooling and job.

When the going gets tough, Connie abandons his young wife. What a setback for Rose of Sharon! Her every ache and worry are compounded. She grows sick and lethargic.

At the boxcar camp some of Rose of Sharon's ailments go away. She gets plenty of rest and nourishing food. But feelings of bitterness over being deserted stay put. Secret jealousy and self-pity keep her from taking part in Al and Aggie's engagement celebration.

As time for the birth approaches, Rose of Sharon does a surprising thing for someone in her delicate state. She insists on picking cotton with the rest of her family. Is she being ruled by a self-destructive impulse? Downhearted people often are. Or might her sudden desire to work be just one of those odd urges that pregnant women feel?

Out in the cotton field she is chilled by the cold and wind. She develops a fever and lies in bed for three days. The next day, as the floodwaters rise around the boxcar, she goes into long and painful labor. The baby is born dead.

Rose of Sharon takes the news stoically, which is unlike her. Maybe she's relieved to know that she won't have to raise a child in awesome poverty. Suffering through childbirth has perhaps opened her eyes. Throughout the book we've seen her concerned almost exclusively with herself and her problems. Now she looks out at the world and turns completely about. In an act of extreme charity, she suckles a dying man with the milk of human kindness.

What Ma learned during months of suffering, Rose of Sharon discovered all at once: everybody must be treated as family if we are to endure. It's a message of love, which Rose of Sharon powerfully dramatizes for us in a barn.

Connie Rivers

Connie is Rose of Sharon's 19-year-old husband. He probably would have been a faithful and affectionate father, but he never got the chance.

He was proud of Rose of Sharon's pregnancy and a little frightened, too. The changes taking place in his young wife happened so quickly they startled him. Like Rose of Sharon, he was obsessed by the baby. He lets the baby rule his thoughts and dreams. Whatever Rose of Sharon might want for the baby, he'll work to get it. First he'll get a house, then a car. He'll get an education and shape a cozy life for his little family.

Connie makes all sorts of plans and promises, in fact, all of which grow further from reality the closer he gets to California. Hooverville is a far cry from the little white house of his dreams. "If I'd of knowed it would be like this I wouldn' of came," he laments to Rose of Sharon.

Disappointments defeat him. Just like that, he walks out on Rose of Sharon and the rest of the Joads.

Pa's comment about his son-in-law could serve as Connie's epitaph: "Connie wasn' no good." He probably didn't deserve a place in a family known for its ability to endure hardship.

Noah Joad

Noah, the first-born son in the Joad family, is a stranger in the world. The night Noah was born, Pa panicked. Terrified by Ma's shrieking, Pa tried to hurry the birth. He pulled at the baby's head, twisting it out of shape.

Noah grew up out of touch with life. He never says much and his face wears a wondering look, as though life is a puzzle that he can't even begin to solve. Yet he learns to read and write, to work and to play, but he just doesn't seem to care. He goes through the motions of living.

When the family finally reaches California, Noah asserts himself for the first time. He's shocked by reports of starving people and doesn't intend to join their ranks. He's going to stay by the river and catch fish. As he tells Tom, "Fella can't starve beside a nice river." So he walks down the river and out of the life of the family. No one seems upset about it, for no one ever really knew him.

Ruthie and Winfield

Ruthie and Winfield are the brats of the family. They're the kind of kids we wish we never had been, but probably were. They have all the qualities that drive parents mad. They're loud, quarrelsome, and moody. Both have an awful lot of growing up to do. Worst of all, they poke each other constantly and get the biggest kick out of tattling on one another.

But they're vulnerable, too. They need love and protection and a pat on the back now and then because life is no easier for them than it is for the older members of the family.

As the youngest in the clan, they're also the most adaptable. They take to life on the road quickly. Migrating to California is an adventure, but filled with sobering experiences like Grampa's death and Casy's arrest.

As mothers will, Ma worries about her two little ones. They seem to be growing up wild, without discipline, without manners or social grace. Ruthie is a particular problem. Joining any group of kids, she's bound to pick a fight. At the government camp she breaks up a game of croquet because she hasn't learned that in a group you have to wait your turn. At the boxcar camp, she gets into a scrap that has serious consequences.

Arguing over a box of Cracker Jack with other kids, Ruthie threatens to get her big brother after one of them. In the heat of the argument, Ruthie reveals that her brother Tom is a killer and is hiding nearby. As a result, Tom must leave the family.

Overall, Ruthie and Winfield weather the hardships of migrant life rather easily. Does their Joad blood give them the capacity to endure? Or is their youth the secret of their success? It's probably a toss-up.

Grampa Joad

Even though Grampa appears only briefly in the book, he leaves a lasting impression. He's a spirited old warhorse with a foul mouth, a fiery temper, and a mischievous glint in his eyes. He does nothing in moderation: he drinks too much, eats too much, and talks all the time.

Some of what he says is nonsense, but some makes a great deal of sense. He's proud to be a Joad and overjoyed to see his favorite grandchild Tom out of prison. "They ain't a gonna keep no Joad in jail," he says.

Grampa, as the oldest Joad, is considered the head of the family, even though everyone recognizes that his mind goes haywire sometimes. At family councils, it's his privilege to speak first.

He has boundless enthusiasm for going west: "Jus' let me get out to California where I can pick me an orange when I want it. Or grapes. . . . I'm gonna squash 'em on my face an' let 'em run offen my chin," he says on the day before the journey begins.

But the next morning he states, "I ain't a-goin'." He demands to be left behind in the country where he feels at home. Although he doesn't say it in words, he is tied to the land of his fathers, and to be wrenched away would break him.

The family must take him anyway. They overpower him by spiking his coffee with medicine. But Grampa never recovers from his stupor. He dies the next day and is buried in a roadside grave. After the makeshift funeral, Casy tells the others, "Grampa didn' die tonight. He died the minute you took 'im off the old place."

Grampa and the land were one and the same. Because the Joads have been transformed from farmers to migrants, Grampa had to die. He had no place in a family that settled in a new place every night.

Granma Joad

Grampa had to have a wife like Granma. She has the same vocabulary, the same spunk, and the same madcap ways as her husband. She needs him to fight with, just as he needs her.

Granma has one unique quality, however. She's ferociously religious. "Pu-raise Gawd fur vittory," she yells when Tom rejoins the family. Granma has gone to prayer meetings where she wailed and moaned for God and Jesus, damned the devil, and shed her sins. She's thrilled to have Casy in her family, even though he professes to have given up preaching. She forces him to say grace at mealtime and to say a prayer over Grampa's grave.

After Grampa dies, she takes ill, never to recover. She dies on the truck while crossing the Mojave Desert, and is buried in California.

Just as Grampa had to die when he left the land, Granma had to die without Grampa. They were two bodies with a single soul. Granma's death also completes the Joads' separation from their old lives.

Muley Graves

When the Oklahoma sharecroppers are evicted from their farms, Muley, the stubborn one, refuses to budge. He's bound to the land where he was born. He'd rather wander the countryside alone, like an "ol' graveyard ghos' " than join the throngs going west.

Muley inspires Grampa Joad's rebellion. Grampa claims that if Muley can stay behind and live off the land, so can he.

One of Muley's casual remarks over a campfire starts Casy thinking about the need for people to share and to work together. Muley doesn't know it, of course, but what he said changes Casy's life, and ultimately the lives of Tom, Ma, and countless others.

Other Elements

SETTING

In some ways *The Grapes of Wrath* is a travel book. In its pages we are taken on a 2000-mile journey from eastern Oklahoma to central California. If you look at a highway map of the Southwest, you can follow the Joads' progress from place to place. Accuracy was important to Steinbeck because he hoped that his book would be more than a piece of fiction; it is meant to be a social document, too.

Because the main characters are sharecroppers turned into migrants, most of the book takes place out-of-doors. So the weather, the land and water, and the road are as important to the novel as almost any character or theme.

The coming of a long drought to America's midsection in the 1930s sets the book into motion. Farmers can't survive on dried-out land. Nor can the banks that own the land make a profit when the tenant farmers don't grow enough to feed even themselves.

In contrast to the parched Dust Bowl, California is fertile and lush. Its orchards and fields grow fruit, nuts, cotton, and vegetables of every sort. It's the Promised Land, the land of milk and honey. It's paradise, except for the people trying madly to keep the migrants at bay. For hundreds of thousands of migrants, including the Joads, of course, California turns out to be a lost paradise.

To be fair, you can't blame only the citizens of California for the migrants' plight. The rains and subsequent floods contribute, too.

The migrant road—Route 66—links Oklahoma to California. Along its miles we see the filling stations, diners, and car lots that line many of America's highways even today. These sites remind us of what our country looks like and repeatedly tell the migrants that they are not wanted—unless they have money.

THEMES

By and large, the major themes in *The Grapes of Wrath* are listed here in the order they show up in the book. It's up to you to decide which are more important than others. Reviewing the text of the novel itself will certainly help.

1. THE BOND BETWEEN LAND AND PEOPLE

Unless you depend on the land for your livelihood, you'll probably never fully understand how strongly a man can be bound to his land. For the tenant farmers of the novel, to be torn away from their land is a shattering experience, akin to death itself. That's why Muley Graves stays behind like a "graveyard ghos' " and Grampa dies shortly after the start of the westward journey.

2. THE EFFECTS OF TECHNOLOGY

Even though *The Grapes of Wrath* takes place in the 20th century, the tenant farmers rely on growing methods of bygone days. That's one reason the farmers are poor and likely to remain so. Because machines can make land profitable, landowning banks send in tractors and dozers. Machine drivers lose touch with the soil; in effect, they become nonhuman pieces of equipment. Without feeling a thing, therefore, they can rumble across the land and knock down anything in their way.

3. CASTING OFF THE OLD WAYS

When the Joads change from farm people to road people, they have to cast off not only many of their belongings, but their habits and customs as well.

Grampa refuses to do it. Ma agonizes over throwing her family letters and clippings into the fire. Casy salts the pork even though it's "women's work." Even the leadership of the Joads must pass to Ma before the family can assume a new identity. It's a painful time for most of them, but the promise of a better tomorrow drives them forward.

4. THE HUMAN FAMILY

People need each other every step of the way. Muley knows he has to share his rabbit with Tom and Casy. The Wilsons can't go on without assistance from the Joads. The Wallaces invite Tom to work with them. Mrs. Wainwright aids Rose of Sharon in childbirth. Rose of Sharon offers her milk to a dying man. You'll have no problem finding many more instances of people helping people in the novel.

5. GOVERNMENT FOR THE PEOPLE AND BY THE PEOPLE

Only in the government camp at Weedpatch do the migrant people find safety and comfort. It's the federal, not the state government that provides refuge. Within the camp itself, people make the rules and select leaders. God helps those who help themselves, the saying goes, but a little help from a benevolent government doesn't hurt.

6. UNIONS

The song "Solidarity Forever" is the anthem of the American labor movement. When workers stick together in a righteous cause, they can accomplish anything. But you have to be prepared to make sacrifices. You can't give in to threats, and above all, you must remain united. If you break with your brother, you'll be hurting both him and yourself.

7. GRAPES OF WRATH
Anger in many guises dominates the book. Why else call it *The Grapes of _Wrath_*? The tenant farmers are angry at the landowners. Roadside characters such as the one-eyed man are angry with themselves. Californians' fear of the migrants turns to anger. And most of all, the migrants are angry. In a land of plenty, they are starving. They should be angry about that, and so should we!

8. QUEST FOR THE DOLLAR
The pursuit of money is a perfectly legitimate activity in our society. But what happens when, in the quest for the dollar, human values are forgotten? Banks force people from their homes; big farmers eat up little farmers; landowners exploit workers; food is burned and buried; people starve. At what point does the pursuit of money turn into a crime?

9. ENDURANCE
The Grapes of Wrath is a story of endurance. You have to marvel at how many of the characters, especially Ma Joad, can put up with such a relentless barrage of trouble, and still go on. Men must be made of sturdy stuff to keep trying in the face of adversity brought on by both nature and other men.

STYLE

It's hard not to be impressed by the richness of language in *The Grapes of Wrath*.

Most of the writing is straightforward narrative prose. But some of the prose is highly poetic, crowded with sensual images ("The dust-filled air muffled sound more completely than fog does") and figures of speech such as metaphors, similes, and personifications ("The full green hills are round and soft as breasts"). Look especially at passages about nature, such as Steinbeck's descriptions of the drought in Chapter 1 and of California springtime in Chapter 25.

An entire chapter turns out to be an extended metaphor. The turtle (Chapter 3) exemplifies endurance and perseverance, qualities that we see demonstrated again and again by the Joads and other migrants.

Steinbeck writes dialogue as the people spoke it. Spelling is unorthodox because the migrant people drop the sounds of certain letters, like the g in words ending in ing, and often slur two words into one, as in Pa'd, meaning Pa would. The people's speech is dappled with expressions such as "a walkin' chunk a mean-mad" and "billy-goatin' aroun'." There's no doubt that the dialogue slows down your reading, but Steinbeck sought the likeness of truth, even though the characters are fictional. Besides, who'd want to read a book about migrants who sound like English teachers?

In some of the interchapters, Steinbeck uses still another style of writing. He bombards you with phrases, bits of spoken conversation, half-thoughts, expressions—a collage of words to give you an impression of a place or an event. You have to fill in the details. For example, what actually happens at the used-car lots (Chapter 7) and in the cotton fields (Chapter 27)?

POINT OF VIEW

Steinbeck wrote *The Grapes of Wrath* during the 1930s, a time of considerable social and economic upheaval in our country. The U.S. was trying to dig itself out of the Great Depression. Franklin D. Roosevelt, president at the time, inspired both undying love and fierce hatred by instituting several social-welfare programs. Most people either supported FDR or considered him an ogre.

Steinbeck belongs in the first group. He's pro-union, pro-welfare, pro-big government. And he tells the tale of the Joads with those biases right out front. We view the world through the eyes of the Joads or, in the interchapters, from the perspective of the mass of migrants. We never hear the other side of the story. Nearly every native Californian we meet is either a deputy, a guard, or a fearful citizen. California seems more like a fascist police state than a piece of the U.S.

Nevertheless, we don't have to think of *The Grapes of Wrath* as just a piece of propaganda, as some people say it is. While the book exposes abuse and suffering of a whole class of people, it also tells an uplifting story of courage and determination. The Joads, in the end, exemplify values that we like to think lie at the root of America's greatness.

FORM AND STRUCTURE

The Grapes of Wrath follows the Joad family for about half a year of their lives. We meet them just after they've been thrown off their land, probably in April or May. We go with them on a long cross-country trek, which lasts, perhaps, slightly more than a month. The last time we see them, they are in a hillside barn seeking refuge from wintry rains and floods, perhaps in November or December. Exact times can't be pinned down.

The Joads' story is told chronologically. Steinbeck occasionally fills in details of the characters' past lives in two ways. Sometimes he just tells us. That's how we learn about Noah Joad's violent birth, for example. Or Steinbeck has characters talk about themselves, as Casy does, or about each other. When Tom tells Casy the story of Uncle John's ill-fated marriage, we listen, too.

Between many of the narrative chapters, Steinbeck inserts interchapters, usually short sketches of economic and social history that bear on the story. Taken all together, the interchapters comprise a colorful background montage of migrant life. (See the accompanying table of chapters and interchapters.)

You can easily divide *The Grapes of Wrath* into three parts. Call the first part Oppression, the time of drought and dust in Oklahoma. The second section, about the journey, can be called Exodus; and the final portion, in California, The Promised Land. In viewing the novel's structure this way, we can discern biblical parallels. The Israelites, God's chosen people, left the land of their bondage, Egypt, and wandered in the desert for many years, searching in vain for a promised land, the land of milk and honey.

THE GRAPES OF WRATH

Narrative Chapters	Interchapters
2. Tom hitches home from prison	1. The dust storms
	3. The turtle
4. Tom meets Jim Casy	5. Foreclosures; tenants versus owners, banks, tractors
6. Tom and Casy meet Muley Graves	
8. Tom is reunited with family	
10. Joads prepare to leave	7. Used-car lots
	9. What to keep, what to sell
13. Journey begins; Joads meet Wilsons; Grampa dies	11. Alienated work; vacant houses
	12. Route 66
16. Car trouble; Ma rebels; Ragged prophet	14. Socialism; "I" versus "we"

The Story

CHAPTER 1

In the opening chapter, Steinbeck takes us to the Dust Bowl, the vast, dried-out farmland of the Southwest in the 1930s. He shows us the gradual bleaching of the land.

What was green and rich and fertile loses its life and turns to dust. Drained of moisture, the red earth turns pink and the gray earth turns to white dust. The wind sweeps the rain clouds away and sends dust billowing into the sky.

Steinbeck then shows us the people. Families worry about the land and crops. The wives worry that their men may crack under the strain. Since the farmers can't fight the weather, they sit silently and hope for rain.

NOTE: This description of the coming of drought is the first of the novel's interchapters. In only a few pages you see the effects of a months-long drought. You are introduced to a motif that will recur as you continue reading, namely, the bond between the land and the people. If land goes bad, life goes bad. But the people are hardy and stoic. They hurt, but they don't break.

The chapter ends in stillness, like the calm before a storm, and in contrast to the start of the next chapter.

CHAPTER 2

A huge shiny-red tractor-trailer, its engine roaring, stands by a roadside diner. Tom Joad, freshly sprung from the penitentiary at McAlester, persuades the trucker to give him a lift, despite the No Riders sign. "Sometimes a guy'll be a good guy even if some rich bastard makes him carry a sticker," says Tom.

How can the trucker refuse to give Tom a ride after such a statement? He wants to be a "good guy" and he certainly wouldn't like to be considered his boss's stooge.

NOTE: The incident tells us something about ties between workers and employers. Doesn't the driver's willingness to pick up Tom suggest that at some point kinship among working people begins to carry more weight than the power of bosses? Steinbeck has begun to develop an idea that later balloons into a major theme in the novel—how working men wield power when they stick together.

Tom's conversation with the driver introduces us to background material about the condition of the land (it's "dusty"), about farmers who have quit (they're "going fast now"), and life on the road (truck drivers become "goddamn sick of goin' "). It also gives the reader a chance to learn about Tom (his father is "a cropper," i.e., a sharecropper), and that Tom is on his way home after serving four years behind bars for homicide.

If we judge Tom by the way he talks to the driver, he seems to have a great big chip on his shoulder. He's coarse and insulting, hardly the kind of fellow you'd like for a traveling companion. Why he berates the truck driver who has done him a favor is unclear. Maybe Tom is just an ungrateful tough guy. On the other hand, his aggressiveness might be explained by his clothes, which brand him as a new ex-con. He knows that people are inquisitive. They probe and sometimes ask embarrassing questions. Acting tough will keep nosy people at a distance.

CHAPTER 3

In this interchapter we watch a land turtle's slow and painful journey through roadside grass, across a highway, and over an embankment. The turtle leaves a beaten trail behind him. Whatever hinders his progress is repelled by his hard shell. A red ant that crawls underneath the shell gets crushed. A woman in a sedan avoids the turtle, but the driver of a pick-up truck swerves to hit him. The wheel nicks the turtle and sends him spinning onto his back. Stopped temporarily, the turtle pauses. After a brief struggle to right himself, he continues his march.

How puzzling to find a chapter about a turtle in *The Grapes of Wrath*. It's different from everything in the novel so far. Let's assume that Steinbeck knows what he's doing, and that he has a sensible plan to fit this turtle into the novel.

In the meantime, it might be worth observing some of the turtle's most apparent qualities. He has tenacity above all: despite obstacles, the turtle drives himself ever forward. He also has endurance, strength, and pride. Steinbeck says the turtle has "hands," and "fierce, humorous eyes," which peer ahead across the road.

Why Steinbeck assigns a turtle characteristics normally reserved for people is an issue worth pondering. If the turtle has symbolic significance, we haven't yet read enough to determine what it may be. Usually we talk of a turtle as an "it." Here Steinbeck uses the pronoun "he." Maybe there's something in that, too.

We'll have to come back to the turtle later.

CHAPTER 4

Out of the truck, Tom removes his shoes. What a joy it is to feel the land under his feet again! As he walks barefoot toward home, he spies a land turtle in the dust and wraps it up in his jacket—a gift for his kid brother. Possibly this is the same turtle we met in the previous chapter.

Later, after Tom meets Jim Casy, the turtle tries to escape. Casy's comment reveals still another quality of turtles: they can't be penned in; they always run off.

Casy compares himself to a turtle. He, too, has "escaped," for he has given up being a preacher. The spirit and "the heart ain't in it," he tells Tom. In former days he howled out the name of Jesus and delighted in baptizing and bringing God to the people. His sermons aroused folks against sin. He aroused himself, too, but in another way. For after his preaching he would grab any willing girl and lay her down in the grass. Is it any wonder he began to feel like a hypocrite? Taking stock of his life, he finally decided that the old-time religion no longer suited him.

Does Casy sound like a philosopher? Although his language is crude, his ideas show that he is a thinker. He's been thinking particularly about his own faith. To Casy, the "Holy Sperit" now means love. Not love of God, however, but love of people. "Why do we got to hang it on God or Jesus?" he asks, "maybe it's all men an' all women . . . , maybe all men got one big soul ever'body's a part of."

What can we make of Casy's words? Tom is a bit embarrassed by them. He's not used to such naked truth. We might conclude that Casy, like Tom, has been released from prison, a prison of fundamentalist religion. But what of that? Again, we probably have to wait until we've read more of the book to understand fully what Casy means.

In contrast, Tom is more interested in down-to-earth matters. He wants to go home to his family, whom he hasn't seen for four years since he was imprisoned for killing a man in a drunken brawl at a dance. As the two men walk along, Tom tells Casy (and the reader, too) a little about his Pa and Ma and other members of the Joad family. When they reach the crest of the hill overlooking the Joad's farm, Tom stops in disbelief. His home has been abandoned.

CHAPTER 5

Why the Joads have deserted their farm becomes apparent in this chapter, a dramatized essay about the economic conflict between the tenant farmers and landowners. Steinbeck uses an imaginary dialogue, with each speaker representing the beliefs of his group. The owners send agents to speak for them. The banks, which Steinbeck aptly calls the Monster, must make a profit, say the agents. If the farmers can't pay, they have to get off the land.

Times are bad; the soil's too dry, the farmers reply.

Then grow cotton!

Can't do that, say the farmers. It'll kill the soil for good.

Too bad, then. Get off the land.

But we've been here for generations. Besides, where'll we go?

That's your problem. Get off!

To make sure the farmers move, the bank sends in bulldozers to knock down the houses. Tractors, like land-eating giants, tear up the land.

The drivers are farmers, too, often friends of the family. Why do they engage in such destructive work? They have to. It's a job, and they need a few dollars to feed their own hungry families.

NOTE: Steinbeck compares the drivers to their machines. In effect, they have become a machine part, no different from a cog or bolt. They lack feeling and sense. They don't think. Perhaps they don't allow themselves to think about their cruel deeds. They have given up their humanity, have sold themselves to the bank and, like the dispossessed farmers, have also become victims of the Monster.

CHAPTER 6

Tom and Casy rummage through the remnants of the Joad farm. Tom thinks Ma may be dead. What other cause would drive his family away?

He is set straight by Muley Graves, a neighbor. The Joads left just two days earlier and have gone to Uncle John's place eight miles away.

Why? The landowners say they can't afford to support small tenant farms any more. Large, mechanized farms might make a profit, so the tenants have been "tractored out."

"How'd my folks go so easy?" inquires Tom. He knows that it's hard to push the Joads around.

What occurred on the Joads' place echoes what we read in Chapter 5. A representative of the land company evicted the Joads. Pa might have shot the man, but the wrong man would be dead. The poor fellow was just doing what he was told.

Then who is responsible?

Why, it's the bank that owns the land, of course.

Who's the bank?

It's not the man behind the desk in the local branch.

Who, then?

Maybe the directors, the stockholders and creditors.

Well, who controls them?

Money. Property. The need to show a profit.

Steinbeck, it seems, has given us a quick lesson in economics, the point being that the Joads and other tenant farmers can't fight back against an adversary that is not a person but an abstraction.

Nevertheless, Muley is engaged in a one-man resistance movement. He has refused to leave. Alone and bitter, he wanders the countryside. He eats small animals and reigns over a dead land. He calls himself a "graveyard ghos'," haunting the empty farms and sometimes playing cat-and-mouse with deputies on their inspection rounds. He thinks that he's slightly touched for living as he does, but the land is his, he's spilled blood on it and, by God, he's going to stay on it. His name fits his personality.

For dinner that evening, the three men share a jack rabbit that Muley has skinned. Muley acknowledges that although he's hungry he obviously must share his catch with Tom and Casy. "I ain't got no choice in the matter," he comments. Casy finds Muley's casual remark rich with implications. "Muley's got a-holt of somepin," says Casy, "an' it's too big for him, an' it's too big for me." All night Casy ponders Muley's big idea. By daybreak Casy has made a decision but, uncharacteristically, he keeps it to himself. We'll have to wait until later to find out what it is.

Conversation over the campfire draws out Tom's private thoughts. How different Tom suddenly seems. His abrasiveness vanishes. There is another side to his personality, after all.

He talks of his crime and punishment. He would kill Herb Turnbull again under the same circumstances. Four years in prison have not changed him. The time has been wasted. It did not feel like punishment. It ought to have had meaning, he says, but it didn't. The senselessness of his imprisonment bothers him. It has made him lose respect for the law and the government.

Tom's words don't seem like the reflections of a hardened criminal. Rather, he's a man with social consciousness. He's thought about society's rules, has found them full of holes, and now feels somewhat bitter.

To add to his resentment, that evening he and his companions hide from the deputy sheriff to avoid being charged with trespassing—on his own land, no less. Tom agrees with Muley that the "On'y kind a gover'ment we got . . . leans on us fellas." His attitude toward authority is important; keep it in mind when in later sections of the book he must decide whether or not to obey the law.

CHAPTER 7

When the impoverished sharecroppers are thrown off their farms, they have to go somewhere. Muley told us in the last chapter that most are headed west to California. But if they don't own a truck or a car, how will they get there? Furthermore, how will they transport their beds and dressers, their pots and kitchen stove?

In this interchapter we see slick, fast-talking used-car salesmen selling worn-out and withered junk-heaps to naïve farmers who know a lot more about mules than about cars.

The farmer has scraped together $50 or $75 and calls on the nearest used-car dealer. He's a welcome sight to the salesman. The farmer is desperate, and the dealer knows it. To clinch a sale, the lot owners lie and cheat. They know that the farmer will be hundreds of miles away before he discovers the leaky radiator or cracked engine block. Although the buyers don't stand a chance in the used-car lot, they have to take it. What other choice do they have?

Shifty used-car salesmen won't be the only people to take advantage of the dispossessed farmers in *The Grapes of Wrath*, but they are among the first.

CHAPTER 8

Picking up the narrative again, Steinbeck takes us to Uncle John's, where we finally get to meet the Joads in person, all three generations of them.

Grampa and Granma are the oldest. Then come Pa and Ma and Uncle John. The next generation includes Tom and his brothers and sisters: Al, Noah, Rose of

Sharon (and her husband, Connie Rivers), Ruthie, and Winfield.

Casy accompanies Tom on the road. He hopes to travel along with the Joads. Can there be any doubt that they will accept him? Although he's another mouth to feed, he's also an able-bodied man and can probably earn his keep. Moreover, the Joads wouldn't turn away their former preacher.

On the way to meet his folks, Tom tells Casy a story about his Uncle John. One day, after four months of marriage, John's young wife complained of stomach cramps. She asked John to call the doctor. He told her that all she needed was some painkiller. The next day, though, the poor girl died of a burst appendix. Is it any wonder, then, that, as Tom says, his uncle is lonely and mean? Later in the book, John goes on drinking sprees. Knowing John's past, you can understand his occasional binges.

Just past sunup Tom and Casy reach John's place. You might think that Tom's family would celebrate the return of the second oldest son. But they don't. The reception, while warm, is not grand. Perhaps the family plight is just too serious at the moment to think of much else. The Joads have been uprooted. They plan to load all their belongings onto an old Hudson and to join the westward migration. They have little money and no real prospects for jobs. Who would not be overcome with worry in such circumstances?

Tom sees his relations one by one. Steinbeck might have shown Tom marching into the thick of the Joads, while, say, the family ate breakfast. Instead, Steinbeck describes Tom's return in another way. Each person greets Tom separately, and we get a glimpse of each member of the family. Let's see what they disclose about Tom's personality.

Pa, whom Tom meets first, is incredulous that Tom is back, but just for an instant. He sees in Tom's return a chance to play a little trick on Ma: he will announce the arrival of a stranger, just to see the look on her face when he recognizes her son.

Ma's reunion with Tom shows a special relationship between mother and son. Tom bites his lip so hard it bleeds. Ma's first words are "Thank God. Oh, thank God." She had been fretting about never seeing Tom again. Ma's response is typical, for she is the family worrier. She carries the family's burdens on her shoulders. She is the healer and the judge. No wonder that Steinbeck calls her the "citadel of the family."

We find that Grampa is a "cantankerous, complaining, mischievous" old man who likes to tell dirty stories. Grampa admires Tom and boasts that no prison is secure enough to hold a Joad. He drinks too much and rarely stops talking or cackling. He bickers constantly with Granma. In spite of his eccentric behavior, though, Grampa is still considered the leader of the Joads. Age, it seems, holds a revered place in their society.

Granma, too, is something of a hellion: crude, loudmouthed, "lecherous," and "savage," hardly the sweet little old grandmother type. Hearing that Tom has returned, she comes out shrieking, "Pu-raise Gawd fur vittory."

But Granma gets a bigger thrill from seeing Casy. Now there can be prayer meetings and proper grace at mealtime. "I ain't a preacher no more," protests Casy. Granma insists anyway that Casy say grace before breakfast. In Granma's eyes, once a preacher, always a preacher.

Casy obliges. He seems to be living up to his vow to love "the people." Casy's prayer is a personal story about how, like Jesus, he went alone into the wilderness and discovered a new religion for himself and the people. It sounds more like a confession, but that doesn't matter to Granma. For her, it's not the content but the ritual that counts. Do you recall that Casy was driven from religion in the first place by that very point of view?

Tom sees his brother Noah. They exchange cool greetings. Noah's behavior is hard to figure out. He seems remote from the family. Later, we find out why Noah is an outsider: he had had a difficult birth, which evidently damaged his brain.

Rose of Sharon, Tom learns, has married and is pregnant. Tom sees her later that day and notices how in four years she has blossomed from a child to a woman. Tom also meets her husband, Connie, a 19-year-old who acts bewildered by the physical changes in his young wife. Both Rose of Sharon and Connie are preoccupied with the coming baby. Their blushes and giggles when they greet Tom suggest just how young they really are.

Twelve-year-old Ruthie and ten-year-old Winfield greet their brother as they would a stranger. They hardly remember him. Four years is a long time in the life of a child.

Al Joad, Tom's other brother, has grown up, too. His main occupation, we discover, is chasing girls. When Tom arrives, Al hasn't yet returned from the previous night's "smart-alecking." We're told that Al has impressed many girls with the information that his brother killed a man in a fight. Evidently, Al is proud of Tom.

For four years Al has filled in for Tom as the family's second son after Noah. How would you expect a person in Al's shoes to react when his older brother returns? If he is disappointed, he doesn't show it. The only thing that bothers him is that Tom hadn't broken out of prison. By waiting until he was paroled, Tom loses face in Al's eyes, and Al loses something to brag about to the girls.

CHAPTER 9

What would it be like to leave your home forever and be allowed to take with you only one full suitcase? What would you choose? What could you do without?

That's the crux of the problem for farm families being evicted from their homes. They have only a small truck or a car to carry all their belongings. What can they do with the things they can't take along? They could leave them behind, of course, or better still, they could sell them. But one man's favorite workhorse is another's worthless old nag. So what do you do? You sell the horse for a fraction of what it is worth. The same is true for the beds, the dressers, the bathtub, and the baby's crib. Nobody wants that old furniture, anyway. So what do you do? You burn it in a big bonfire. Wouldn't it hurt you terribly to see the things you love go up in smoke?

NOTE: Steinbeck's interchapter prepares us for what the Joads will be doing in the next chapter. We'll see their pain as they cast away everything that won't fit in their truck.

CHAPTER 10

If you're a sensitive person and about to leave the country of your birth forever, how might you feel? A bit sad, perhaps?

Most people would also be a little fearful of what the future might bring. Your uncertainty would be still stronger if you were about to travel 2000 miles because someone showed you a handbill on yellow paper saying that workers were needed to pick peaches, oranges, and grapes in California. On the other hand, you might also look forward to a new life in a better place.

That's Ma's mixed state of mind when the chapter opens. She tells Tom her fears. As a good son, what might Tom do? He could try to reassure her, tell her not to worry. But Tom is too honest for that. He says that "a fella from California" has told him that "they's too many folks lookin' for work right there now. An' he says the folks that pick the fruit live in dirty ol' camps an' don't hardly get enough to eat. He says wages is low an' hard to get any."

If Tom's information is correct, no one with a grain of sense would want to go to California. But since there's no place else for the Joads, Ma replies, "Oh, that ain't so." She denies it. What else can she do at this point? She also takes heart from Tom's advice to live one day at a time, a lesson he taught himself in prison.

Because Ma must prepare for the journey, she doesn't have enough time to fret, anyway. We know, however, that despite the optimistic face she shows to her family, Ma is worried.

To add to her worries, Pa, Uncle John, and Al return from town with just $18 to show for the sale of the Joads' horse, wagon, farm implements, and furniture. The three men are upset and angry. They sold too cheaply.

The last thing the Joads need now is car trouble. But suddenly, Al Joad, the family auto mechanic, announces that the old Hudson truck he bought has sprung a leak in the radiator and needs new brakes.

And to make matters still worse, the family learns that by leaving the state of Oklahoma, Tom will be breaking his parole. If caught, he would be sent back to McAlester for three more years. What should a man do in such circumstances? Let his family go alone? Stay behind and wander the countryside like Muley Graves? Or should he take a chance? Tom, it turns out, doesn't give the problem a second thought. His family needs him. Besides, the law has let him down in the past. Why should he begin to respect it now? He pledges to Ma that he will stay out of trouble, but as soon as he crosses the state line, Tom will become a fugitive.

When the Joads are beset with troubles, they call a meeting. Everyone knows where to sit: men huddle in the center, women behind them, children in the outer circle. Grampa, as the oldest, has the first word, even though his mind has gone silly. Anyone can talk, but decisions are made by the men.

In two ways this night's meeting differs from those of the past. Instead of assembling in the house, the family meets alongside the truck, which has suddenly become the Joads' "place." (The Joads, it seems, are being transformed from a "home" family into a "road" family.) Also for the first time, Al Joad joins the nucleus of men. As the family mechanic, he has earned a spot in the center. He reports on the condition of the truck: she's okay—weak, but she'll make it. On the road he'll be responsible for keeping the old Hudson rolling.

Then the group takes up Casy's request to join the family. Can they afford to feed still another person? Ma speaks up: "It ain't kin we? It's will we?" Adding that no Joad has ever refused food and shelter or a lift on the road to anyone who asked, Ma prevails. Casy is taken into the family. Have you noticed that Ma's authority has begun to creep into the family's decision-making?

If you've ever left home for any length of time, you're probably familiar with the feeling of restlessness most people feel before a trip. You're keyed up, you can't sleep, and time seems to pass oh, so slowly. You can't wait to get started. The same sense of urgency about getting underway hits the Joads that night. They decide to leave the next day instead of waiting.

Their night is filled with bustle. Slaughter the pigs and salt the meat. Collect tools from the barn, pack the clothes in boxes, gather pots and utensils from the kitchen. Load the truck. Make it even down below. Fill in the spaces with blankets. Throw the mattresses on top. If you don't need it, don't take it; we don't have much room!

Ma lets Casy salt the pork, and she retreats alone into the empty house. She finds her box of old family letters, clippings, and photographs. We see her holding it in her lap for a long time and remembering the years gone by. Then, biting her lip to keep from weeping, Ma places the collection gently into the stove. The flames lick up and over the box. For Ma, the past is over. Only the present counts now. By daybreak, the Joads are ready to go. All but one Joad, at any rate. At the last moment Grampa announces, "I jus' ain't a-goin'." His reason is simple: "This here's my country. I b'long here." Grampa's rebellion may have been triggered by the sudden appearance of Muley Graves, come to bid the Joads goodbye, but can Grampa survive like Muley? The family thinks not. They devise a plan to spike Grampa's coffee with a "soothin' syrup." It works. Soon Grampa falls asleep and is hoisted onto the truck like a piece of baggage.

As the sun rises, the Joads' truck, groaning under its load, crawls slowly (like a turtle) onto the highway going west.

CHAPTER 11

What happens to land when it is left vacant? What happens to empty houses? What happens to the vitality of a place when the people leave and machines take over?

This interchapter draws an analogy between abandoned farmland and death. When people occupy the land and the day's work is done, the heat and smell of life remain. When the tractor driver turns off his machine and goes home to town, a corpse is left behind.

Forsaken houses fall prey to the wind and wild things. Little boys hurl stones through the windows. Paint flakes off, and wind tears away the shingles. Bats and mice take up residency. Weeds spring up where they had never grown before.

NOTE: This grim portrait of the dead land brings us to a juncture in the novel. We've seen the conditions that forced the farmers out of their homes. Now we'll see what these new migrants face along the road.

CHAPTER 12

If you look at an old highway map of the western United States, you'll find Route 66 cutting through Oklahoma, the Texas panhandle, bisecting New Mexico and Arizona, and reaching Needles, California. The road then crosses the Mojave Desert and enters the lush valleys of central California. (Parts of Route

66 fell into disuse and were abandoned in the 1970s and early 80s.)

Steinbeck calls 66 the "road of flight." In the 1930s swarms of migrants rode it out of the Dust Bowl. They came from little no-name places and joined the westward tide. The highway became a river of people.

Along its miles, day after day, thousands of dramas were played. Each was unique, but each became part of the great pattern of life on the road.

No driver likes car trouble, especially when he's trying to make good time and he's got a huge cargo aboard. But those old jalopies crowding the highway broke down again and again. Repairs were expensive. A day lost fixing an engine meant a day's delay in finding work in California.

Throughout this chapter, Steinbeck lets us hear the conversations of scared and angry men talking inside their cars, at repair shops, and at filling stations. They talk mainly of gaskets and hoses and con-rods, of tires and overheated engines. Then there's talk of California. Will they ever get there? They hear rumors now and then about border patrols at the California state line turning people back. They don't want any more poor people messing up their beautiful state.

Sometimes a car can't be fixed. What do the people do then? Do they walk? Where do they get the courage to keep going? There's one inspiring story circulating among the migrants about a stranded family of twelve being picked up by some rich fellow and being driven and fed all the way to California. Most stories you hear, however, end in despair.

CHAPTER 13

The Joads cover 200 miles the first day. By sundown we have met one of many roadside characters who, in contrast to the Joads, have failed to endure life's hardships. We see the family dog crushed by a speeding car. We also meet Sairy and Ivy Wilson, a couple from Kansas with a disabled car and a belief in charity for all. That night Grampa Joad dies in the Wilsons' tent and later is buried wrapped in Sairy's quilt. His death creates a tight bond between the two families.

That Grampa dies so soon comes as no surprise. Casy explains why: "Grampa an' the old place, they was jus' the same thing." Removing him from the land was like pulling his plug. With the connection broken, the old man lost his will to live, and he dies quickly of a stroke.

Grampa's death makes sense. He's a superfluous member of the family. In the days when Grampa was in charge, the Joads had been a stable farm family. Now they are starting over as a road family. For the younger members of the group, life holds endless potential. Look at Rose of Sharon and Connie, for example. They are totally absorbed in their unborn baby, the next generation of Joads. They see a sleek Lincoln Zephyr glide by on the highway and talk of owning a car like that some day, but only after they buy a house for the baby to grow up in. Once in California, Connie will go to school and get a good job. Rose of Sharon will raise the baby in a little white house with a picket fence. The two of them are caught up in their private American dream.

Their dream may seem unreal to you. It should; life is not a fairy tale. But compare it to Grampa's vision of the future. To him California meant squeezing grapes over his head and letting the juice trickle down through his whiskers. Did Grampa know he talked nonsense? Dying on the first day hints strongly that he did.

If the youngest Joads are meant to dream, and the oldest to die, what's left for the middle generation— for Ma, Pa, Uncle John, and also Tom and Casy? Ma thinks her function is to keep the family going. She tells Al Joad, "That's all I can do. I can't do no more." Let's see how true Ma is to her word in the remainder of the chapter. When Al suggests that maybe they shouldn't have brought the preacher, Ma prophesies that Casy will help the family sometime. (Whether Casy will give the kind of help Ma needs remains to be seen.) At a roadside stop, Ma helps Granma relieve herself in the bushes (physical help). She comforts Rose of Sharon, shaken by the sight of their dog hit by a car (emotional help). Later, she fixes the food, prepares Grampa's body for burial, and agrees to ally the Joads with the Wilsons. "Each'll help each, an' we'll all git to California," she says. By the time she lays her head down to sleep, Ma has put in a solid day's work in behalf of her family.

Earlier in the day, Al pulls the Hudson into a filling station. The owner is hostile to the Joads. They aren't welcome unless they can buy gas. "Think we're beggin'?" says Al, pulling out his money. The fat owner quickly changes his attitude and nervously explains his suspicions. People "come in, use water, dirty up the toilet, an' then, by God, they'll steal stuff an' don't buy nothin'." The sweat-soaked fat man has no sympathy for the hordes of people going west. They puzzle him. "What they gonna do?" he asks. "I don't know what the country's comin' to."

Casy, ever willing to extend himself, tries to explain what, in fact, the country's comin' to: "People moving . . . 'cause they want somepin better'n what they got. An' that's the on'y way they'll ever git it." The man doesn't listen. He takes up his lament again: "I don't know what the country's comin' to."

Irritated, Tom tells off the fat man. "You ain't askin' nothin'; you're jus' singin' a kinda song." He scolds the man for doing nothing to improve his own lot. "Country's movin' aroun', goin' places. They's folks dyin' all aroun'. Maybe you'll die pretty soon, but you won't know nothin'."

Neither Tom nor Casy has anything to gain from trying to set the fat man straight. Why do they bother, then? Maybe each believes that life can be better, but only if you make it so. If you don't keep trying, you're licked. What bestows meaning on life is the effort you put into it. In short, Tom and Casy are trying to save the fat man from himself. They're crusaders, especially Casy, who says, "Here's me that used to give all my fight against the devil. . . . But they's sompin' worse'n the devil got hold a the country, an' it ain't gonna let go till it's chopped loose." Exactly what Casy thinks has snared the country is hard to tell at this point, but he gives the impression that he's going after it with the same fervor he once used to chase sinners.

Before he can devote himself entirely to his new cause, however, Casy has one more duty to perform in the old way. Realizing that her husband is dying, Granma insists that Casy say a proper prayer. Casy recites the Twenty-third Psalm. It seems that Casy won't be free to pursue his new religion of the people until the old generation is dead and buried.

Grampa's burial becomes a practical problem. What should be done with the body? The law says report the death and pay the undertaker forty dollars. But if your entire family fortune is less than two-hundred dollars, you may look for another way. They decide to bury Grampa on their own. In case the authorities find the grave, they will include a note in a bottle explaining the circumstances of the death and burial.

A time of grief often knits people together. As Grampa lays dying in the Wilsons' tent, the Joads and Wilsons, strangers that morning, become neighbors in the afternoon, and friends in the evening. Before the night is over, the two families will unite, for each can gain from being with the other. Al will fix the Wilsons' car. Some of the Joads will ride in it, lightening the load on the Hudson.

CHAPTER 14

Simply stated, the point of this interchapter is that "the times, they are a-changin'." That, however, may be the only simple thing about this profound and poetic piece of *The Grapes of Wrath*.

To understand the upheaval going on in the country, let's take the chapter one step at a time:

1. The owners of the western lands feel uneasy about changes taking place among the working people. Militant workers are forming labor unions. New taxes and government regulations that aid the working class make the wealthy owners nervous, too. (Remember, we're in the 1930s, the time of the Great Depression and FDR's New Deal.)

2. The landowners protect themselves because they feel threatened by the changes. (We'll see how they do it in subsequent chapters.)

3. Regardless of what the landowners do, however, they can't stop the changes, largely because they misunderstand their origin and don't understand the power that brought them into being in the first place. The holders of land are doing battle with the unions and the labor laws. But, says Steinbeck, they're fighting the wrong enemy. The real adversary is the set of conditions that led to the formation of unions and the writing of laws to protect the workers—such things as hunger, the desire for a decent life, and above all, the capacity of men to believe in a cause and, if necessary, to suffer and die for it.

4. What is this irrepressible cause that drives workers on and on? Steinbeck calls it "Manself." To understand Manself, think of something you've done that made you feel proud. Let's say, for instance, that you got a good grade on an exam. The effort you put into the test was paid back to you in the admiration you received. But beyond the praise, you made a greater gain. You grew in stature as a human being. That is, you did something that only humans can do, thereby making yourself more human. That capacity to grow "beyond your work" is, in Steinbeck's words, Manself.

You might well ask what Manself has to do with the Joads and Casy and the rest of the migrants, whom we left in a roadside camp somewhere between Oklahoma and California. Surely Manself is not a concept they would put into words. Yet a desire to create a dignified life, fit for humans, drives them on. Would they suffer and die for it? We'll have to bide our time to find out.

5. In pursuit of a life of dignity, outcast migrant families have discovered a way to make the road less rocky. People form alliances, both formal and informal. We saw the Joads and the Wilsons coalesce in the last chapter. I (singular) became we (plural), and both parties were the better for it.

Fusion puts an end to loneliness, fear, and suspicion. Sharing a campsite leads to sharing food, and maybe sharing the children's toys. Then there's sharing of stories and problems. That's it! That's the key! Together people solve problems they couldn't begin to tackle alone. They suddenly take control of their lives. They've gained power.

Taken as a whole, then, what messages does this complex chapter convey? To the landowners, it's a warning to watch out for the approaching revolution. To the great mass of people, it's a hymn in praise of solidarity. To us, the readers, it's a hint of things to come in the novel.

CHAPTER 15

We're back on the road again. America is on the move in this interchapter. Cars and trucks from every state whisk along Route 66. Now we are pulled into one of hundreds of indistinguishable roadside diners where the waitress' name is always Mae and the boss is always Al. We overhear conversations at the counter. What people talk about is what you'd expect—virtually everything. It's small talk over coffee or a Coke, jokes, anecdotes, a bit of teasing, chit-chat about the weather, and lots of scornful remarks about the steady stream of migrants' cars and trucks rolling wearily by day after day.

An overloaded '26 Nash car stops. The man of the family asks to buy bread. Mae says, "This ain't a grocery store. We got bread to make san'widges." But Al, sympathetic with the poor man, orders Mae to sell a loaf of bread. Mae follows Al's lead and accepts only a penny for two candy sticks that really cost five cents each. Bill, the trucker observing the incident, knows charity when he sees it. He leaves a tip for Mae many times the amount of the check.

Much later in the novel Ma Joad observes that poor people rarely get help from the well-to-do. It's ordinary people who'll more often lend a hand. Don't Al and Mae and Bill confirm Ma's observation?

CHAPTER 16

The Hudson and the Dodge—no longer the Joads' Hudson and the Wilsons' Dodge, but a small caravan belonging to both families—plod slowly westward across Texas.

Travelers often get into a groove. If you've driven for days on a long trip, you'll recognize these symptoms: nothing matters but movement; you mark time in miles; eating and sleeping routines change; even when you stop, the hum of the engine lingers in your ears.

The Joads have acquired the momentum of life on the road. The youngest, Ruthie and Winfield, adapt first. Then the older ones. All but Granma, in fact, who has fallen ill and seems to have taken leave of her senses. She bays like a "houn' dog," as Al Joad says, "an' don' seem to reco'nize nobody." She's showing signs that she may soon follow Grampa to the grave.

To pass the time, Rose of Sharon and Connie imagine how lovely life will be in California. Ma can't participate in their imaginings. She seems to know it is all a dream. Does that mean she's a realist? Possibly, but not altogether, because she has visions of her own. She aims to keep the family intact, come what may. "It ain't good for folks to break up," she tells Rose of Sharon. A short time later she makes the point vividly, by threatening to strike with a jack handle anyone who defies her.

How does Ma get into such a state? It's so unlike her. Her outburst has its origin in car trouble. The Dodge breaks a con-rod, which will take a good day or more to repair. Tom and Casy propose to fix it while the truck goes on ahead. In the Dodge, they can make good time and will catch up in a few days. Does the idea make sense? It does to everyone but Ma. She can think of a dozen ways in which Tom and Casy will fail to rejoin the family. "I ain't a-gonna go," she says.

"What you mean, you ain't gonna go? You got to go," Pa argues. "We [the men] made up our mind."

Ma is relentless. She brandishes the jack handle. "On'y way you gonna get me to go is to whup me."

Ma's revolt astonishes Pa. He knows that if he gives in, he will have abdicated his traditional role as head of the family. It's a big step, but he takes it, convinced that Ma's opinion—that "All we got is the family unbroke"—is correct.

Back home, Pa couldn't have done it. Out on the highway, however, a new set of rules has gone into effect. The family, having witnessed Ma's coup, realizes that the old ways just don't count anymore.

Ma takes over immediately. She makes a plan for the family to stop at the next roadside campsite and wait for the car to be fixed.

From now on we'll have to consider Ma the leader of the Joads, and her principal belief—that at all costs the family must stick together—as the Joads' eleventh commandment.

Tom Joad swings into the task of taking out the damaged con-rod. He knows what he's doing. Unlike most skillful mechanics, Tom does the work adroitly and can talk about other things at the same time. He and Casy speculate on what their future might be like. Tom avoids looking too far ahead. He clings to what he learned in prison: "I'm jus' puttin' one foot in front a the other."

Casy, on the other hand, sees the big picture. "They's stuff goin' on that the folks doin' it don't know nothin' about—yet," he says, referring to the flood of west-bound migrants. "They's gonna come a thing that's gonna change the whole country." Do Casy's words sound familiar? They should, because they resound with themes introduced in Chapter 14.

Al Joad returns with the truck and picks up Tom. En route to the auto junkyard, Al quizzes Tom about prison life and tries to talk of personal family matters. Tom won't do it. "I ruther not," Tom says. "I ruther jus'—lay one foot down in front a the other." Why is Tom so reticent? Why is it painful for him to talk of anything except the here and now? Did his time in prison rob him of the capacity to feel? Evidently not, considering what happens in the junkyard.

The yardkeeper, a one-eyed man who hates his boss intensely, lets Tom and Al rummage around. They get lucky and soon find the part they need. In the meantime, the one-eyed man, his empty eye socket squirming with muscles, berates his boss and weeps in self-pity. Tom turns on the man: "Now look-a-here fella. You got that eye wide open. An' ya dirty, ya stink. Ya jus' askin' for it. Ya like it. Lets ya feel sorry for yaself." Tom then tells the man a story of a one-legged whore who did a brisk business by capitalizing on her defect instead of giving in to it.

NOTE: The point of Tom's story is lost on the man, but presumably not on the reader. The tale is a parable, a story from which one learns a lesson. Tom wants to help the man, to help him see the possibilities of life more clearly, in spite of having only one eye. Although Tom treats the man roughly, he is not without feeling. His words disclose a profound concern for others, especially for downtrodden, defeated people. Remember the fat man at the filling station? You might disapprove of Tom's tactlessness, but can you give Tom credit anyway, for his intent?

More and more, we are discovering the depths of the real Tom Joad. Rather than jabber about the future or reminisce about the past, Tom is a man of action. When something needs doing, he does it. Think, for example, of the alacrity with which he fixes the car. Casy talks about loving all the people; Tom acts on the idea. If you consider Casy the teacher, think of Tom as the star pupil, demonstrating in his own way what he has been taught.

Even though Tom prefers to "lay one foot down at a time," he runs headlong into the future that very night after the family has reassembled at a camp-ground.

The owner calls the migrants "bums." As you might expect, Tom bristles, but aside from a few sarcastic retorts, he keeps his cool. He also hears for the first time that vagrancy laws have been toughened up, just to keep the migrants on the move. The most troubling indication of things to come, however, is a story told about California by a ragged man huddled with other migrant men around a campfire.

When the ragged man announces, "I'm comin' back. I been there," the men's faces quickly turn toward him. "I don' wanna fret [worry] you," he says, but then he proceeds to tell a woeful tale. He's lost a wife and two children to starvation in California. The authorities didn't care. They just listed the deaths as heart failure.

"You'll be a-campin' by a ditch, you an' fifty other families," the ragged man says, and when you've got nothing left to eat and you're willing to work for pennies a day, you'll be invited to pick peaches or to chop cotton. For every job three times as many starving workers show up as they can use. Naturally, they hire those who'll work for the least pay. So, "lemme tell ya what to do when ya meet that fella says he got work.

Ast him to write down what he's gonna pay. Ast him that. I tell you men you're gonna get fooled if you don't."

Bad news—even when it's the truth—is never welcome. Most of the men around the fire consider the ragged man a troublemaker and a shiftless bum. "You sure you ain't a labor faker?" asks the campground owner, suggesting to the others that the man has been sent to stir up discontent.

Later, Pa almost tells Ma the ragged man's story. But Tom intervenes. He's decided to keep it from her. If the story is true, what can she do about it, anyway? To turn back is out of the question. The Joads—like the turtle left behind many pages ago—must go on.

CHAPTER 17

Here's a fact you can depend on: When people get together for a length of time, sooner or later they're going to develop customs, a pattern of behavior, and a set of rules to live by. You can probably observe this in your classes. Doesn't each class have a personality? Can't you expect certain things to happen each time you walk into the room?

The migrant families in *The Grapes of Wrath* had certain expectations, too, when they pulled into roadside migrant camps each night. Steinbeck tells us about the pattern of life in the camps in this interchapter.

Every night small, temporary societies took shape. The people changed, but not the rules, rights, and customs. Twenty families became one family, drawn together by loneliness and confusion. All came from a place of sadness; all were headed toward a place of hope.

No one told them what they had to do. They did it because their survival depended on it. You can't foul the drinking water, for example. And you can't intrude on others' privacy. You can't flaunt good, rich food in front of neighbors who are famished. Rules were unspoken, but they carried the force of law. If you couldn't follow them, even after a warning, you were beat up or cast out of the society.

After each day's traveling, families unfolded in the camps. Everyone did his or her job: setting up the tent, going for water and firewood, tending the sick, fixing the evening meal, washing up. Then there was time to visit, to discover your neighbors, talk of land and homes left behind and of tomorrow's hopes.

By sunup, the camping place was vacant again, waiting for the arrival of the next night's tenants.

CHAPTER 18

At the Arizona state line, the Joads meet their first border guard. The Joads enter Arizona on the condition that they "keep movin'." They do, and finally reach the edge of California. Still to go before they reach the fertile central valleys where workers are needed is the great Mojave Desert. But first they need a rest, and so they pull into a campsite near a flowing river. By the time the Joads break camp later that day, the family will have been altered again.

NOTE: Today, if you travel a major highway there are no guards anywhere, but in the 30s state troopers were placed at border crossings to check the migrants' vehicles for undesirable plants and people. If they didn't like your looks, you were turned away.

To cool off, the Joad men bathe in the river. Two fellow bathers, men on their way back home to Oklahoma, confirm what the ragged man had said: You can't make a living in California.

The two men have decided to return to Oklahoma because it's better to starve to death with friends than with people who hate them. One of them explains: The land in California is pretty as can be, but you can't have any of it. You can't even stop on it, even though it's not being used. That'll make you angry, but what will make you still angrier is the hateful look on people's faces.

Why do Californians hate you? Because they're scared of you. They know that if you're starving you'll do anything to get food. Three-hundred thousand hungry people can stir up a lot of fright, so the deputy sheriffs push you around, and the people call you "Okie" and do everything they can to make you want to go back where you came from.

What a dilemma for the Joads. They can't go back. Yet to go forward could be even worse.

Nevertheless, they must go ahead. "We're a-goin' there, ain't we?" asks Uncle John. "None of this here talk gonna keep us from goin' there." All agree but Noah, the strange firstborn son of the Joads. The prospect of starving in California frightens him so badly that he decides to abandon the family. He'll take his chances by the river, catching fish, making his way in life alone.

You might expect Noah's departure to surprise the family. It doesn't. It was almost expected because, as Tom says, Noah was "a funny kind a fella." But to Ma, Noah's leaving signifies the start of what she hoped would never happen—the break-up of the family.

And a short time later another piece of the "family" breaks off. Sairy Wilson can't go on. She's too sick and weak from a disease that sounds much like cancer, although neither she nor anyone else in the story ever says so. The Wilsons stay behind when the Joads turn westward again.

It's odd, isn't it, that Ma, the mainstay of the Joads, is still unaware of what her menfolk have heard about what awaits them down the road. She gets her first taste of abusive treatment, however, while the men are bathing. While Ma tends to Granma, ailing in the tent, a uniformed trooper barges in. "You can't stay here," he tells Ma. "You're in California, an' we don't want you goddamn Okies settlin' down." Ma is about to smash the man with a skillet, but the word "Okie" stops her cold. It puzzles her, and later makes her weep. Ma has been initiated to life in "the land of milk and honey."

While in the tent, Ma has still another unwelcome caller. Having heard that Granma lay dying, a Jehovite woman stops in. The woman wants to hold a prayer meeting for Granma. Ma resists. Not only is Granma too weak to put up with the howling and jumping of the Jehovites, but Ma no longer has use for the rites and customs of church-going. Casy's philosophy has evidently made a dent in Ma's thinking. Like Tom, Ma may soon be a disciple of Casy's beliefs.

With prospects grimmer than ever before and three fewer people in their company, the Joads move on toward the feared desert crossing. They must cross at night. Daytime temperatures reach 120 degrees. Last stop before the Mojave is Needles, California. As the Joads pull away from the gas pumps, we are privy to a brief conversation between the service-station attendants:

"Jesus, I'd hate to start out in a jalopy like that."

"Well, you and me got sense. Them goddamn Okies got no sense and no feeling. They ain't human. . . . They ain't a hell of a lot better than gorillas."

If such a comment is typical of what Californians think, how can poor migrant families expect to achieve their dreams of a good, decent life in the Golden State? But a still more pressing question is, how will they survive there?

Crossing the desert takes all night. Connie and Rose of Sharon make love on top of the truck. In the cab, Uncle John confides in Casy. He's trying to figure things out, once and for all. He's not sure, for example, whether he's a help or hindrance to the family. He doesn't know whether he sinned when he let his wife die. Casy gives John advice but no answers. John, like the rest of us, will have to find answers on his own.

Meanwhile, on the back of the truck, Ma lies on the mattress next to Granma. The old woman sleeps fitfully. Ma tries to comfort her: "It's gonna be all right. You know the family got to get acrost [the desert]." Approaching the western edge of the Mojave, the truck must stop for an agricultural inspection. An official orders the truck unloaded. Ma protests, "I swear we ain't got anything! I swear it. An' Granma's awful sick." Ma's intense plea startles her family. A quick look at Granma convinces the officer to let the truck pass. "You can get a doctor in Barstow. That's only eight miles."

In Barstow Ma protests again. "She's awright—awright. Drive on. We got to get acrost." Again, the family puzzles over Ma's peculiar behavior. Is Granma all right or isn't she?

Finally, when the desert lies behind them we learn the truth. Granma is dead. To keep the family going Ma had lain all night next to Granma's body. As she looks around at the great flat valley, green and beautiful, spread out before them, Ma knows she's accomplished her goal. She got Granma to "lay her head down in California," and she got her family across.

NOTE: If you ever doubted Ma's strength, doubt no longer. She'll do anything—literally anything—for her family. In fact, the Joads look in awe at Ma's self-sacrifice. Casy observes in wonder, "There's a woman so great with love—she scares me."

CHAPTER 19

We've reached another turning point in the book. The journey is over. We've made it to the Promised Land—California.

It's a big state, one of the biggest. It's got lots of land. Since it's so big, how come there's so little of it for the quarter-million newcomers from the Dust Bowl? Steinbeck gives us his answers in this inter-chapter.

But first he gives us history. Initially, Mexico owned the land. Then the squatters arrived and laid claims to the land. After a time, loving the earth and growing things on it were not enough for the owners. Passion for the soil turned to lust for money. The owners had to be businessmen, too. Good businessmen ate up the bad ones and farming became an industry. Farms grew larger and owners fewer. The few owners no longer worked the land. They hired foremen and brought in immigrants to work for peons' wages. The owners farmed not on land but in ledgers.

Now came the threat. Hungry, dispossessed farmers from the Dust Bowl sought homes in a new place. No matter where they came from, they were called "goddamn Okies," and they were out to seize land. The owners hated them because they were fierce and frightening. The storekeepers hated them because they had no money, and the laboring people hated them because they worked for less and took away jobs.

The word went out: Keep the Okies down or they'll take over the country. Keep 'em in line or Christ only knows what they'll do. Make 'em live in Hoovervilles—little temporary towns of tents, cardboard shacks, and weedy enclosures. Send in the deputies once in a while to keep 'em in line. Get tough with 'em. Treat 'em rough. Scare 'em. Even burn their towns down. Hoovervilles are a menace to public health, anyway. We gotta keep the goddamn Okies movin' 'cause if they ever get together there ain't nothin' that'll stop 'em.

And that's the way it is in California when the Joads arrive.

CHAPTER 20

Granma's body is taken to the coroner in town and, for a five-dollar fee, buried in the local potter's field. With about forty dollars left in the world, the Joads will almost literally start from scratch in California.

Their first objective: find work. How do you find work in a strange place? There are no employment agencies or classified ads for migrant laborers. So you get a job the old-fashioned way—by good luck or by asking around.

Driving out to the country, the family sees a settlement of tents and shacks, and prepares to camp for the night. The place is a mess. As Steinbeck tells us, it's "hung with slovenly repair." Welcome to Hooverville, Joads!

NOTE: Why *Hoover*-ville? Hundreds of rundown, rusted, litter-strewn towns of poor people were named with bitter humor in "honor" of President Herbert Hoover, the person widely held responsible for leading the U.S. into the Great Depression.

Once the Joads' tent is up, Ma prepares to cook a stew for the family. The smell of cooking attracts a ragged crew of children, who gather around the fire hoping for a handout. The children are hungry, but there's only enough stew for the family. What is Ma to do? Feed the children and deny her family, which she values more than anything in the world? Whatever she decides, someone will go hungry.

Forced to make the painful choice, she doles out small portions to her family and leaves the near-empty stew pot for the children to scrape out. Moments later, however, her kindness backfires. The mother of a little boy storms over to Ma. "You kin he'p me by mindin' your own children an' lettin' mine alone." Her voice shakes with fury. "Don' you go a-boastin' and a-braggin' about havin' stew. Don' you do it. I got 'nuf troubles 'thout that."

If you've ever had a generous gesture of yours misinterpreted, you'll understand Ma's feeling of helplessness as the angry woman stalks away. Next time Ma feels the impulse to help a stranger, she may think twice. On the other hand, we know that she probably won't be deterred by one setback.

In the meantime, Tom tours Hooverville and stops to talk with Floyd, a young resident of the town. Floyd hands Tom about the worst piece of news imaginable. There's no work to be had around here. As

soon as he can grind his car's valves, Floyd aims to
drive out of the area. Maybe north, where there's a
rumor of jobs.

Everything else that Floyd tells Tom is discourag-
ing, too. When there is work a hundred men show up
for a single job, lured by the promise of a decent
wage. But the employers break their word and offer
much less. If you refuse to work for a pitiful fifteen
cents an hour, that's your problem. When your kids
are hungry, though, and you're out of gas, you have
no choice, do you?

Twice, we learn later, Floyd has been deceived by
the promise of good pay. He advises Tom not to
waste gas going to a work site unless he's signed a
contract with the hiring agent for a set wage.

Another thing: When fruit ripens, it must be picked
immediately. So, the orchards hire hundreds of workers for a week or two. When picking's over, they don't
want you hanging around. They kick you out and
move you along.

Tom has a thought about the ripe fruit. If all the
workers got together and refused to work for low pay,
the fruit would rot. "Wouldn' be long 'fore the price
went up, by God!"

Tom is talking about a strike, of course. A strike
may be a new idea to Tom, but not to Floyd, who lists
all the tactics that the owners are using to keep workers in line. They throw strike leaders in jail. They place
"stools" [stool pigeons] in the migrant camps to report
troublemakers. Talk out of turn and you're blacklist-
ed; you'll never work again.

By now we know Tom well enough to predict his
reaction. True to form, Tom vows not to let himself be
pushed around. But if you get tough with a cop, Floyd

tells him, you'll end up dead in a ditch. If Tom knows what's good for him, he'll keep his mouth shut—no matter how hard it may be to do so.

We don't have to wait long for Tom's self-control to be tested. Two official-looking men—a contractor and a deputy sheriff—drive into the camp and announce the need for fruit pickers in Tulare County. Floyd speaks up. He wants to know if the men are hiring the pickers or just collecting as many as they can. He also demands to know the wage they'll pay. The men don't like Floyd's attitude. "He's talkin' red, agitating trouble," one says to the other. They invent a reason to arrest Floyd: he looks like someone who broke into a used-car lot in town last week.

Angrily, Tom interferes. "You got nothin' on him," he says. The deputy tells Tom to keep his "trap shut" and orders Floyd into the car.

Suddenly, Floyd smashes the deputy with his fist and makes a break for it. Tom trips the deputy and sends him sprawling. The deputy pulls a gun. He takes aim at Floyd, but Casy steps from the crowd and knocks the man out with a kick in the neck.

The residents of Hooverville know that this incident will provoke some retaliation. The place will be burned to the ground. Tom is in danger of being arrested for helping Floyd. In the heat of the moment, he had evidently forgotten his own status as a fugitive. Or had he? Possibly he's already driven by the impulse to help others, even if he pays the price of his own freedom.

But it's Casy who goes to jail. As the police sirens approach the camp, Casy decides to take the blame for Tom. "I ain't doin' nothin' but set aroun'," he says. The family needs Tom, but it doesn't need him. Anyway, he owes the Joads for bringing him along to California. All these arguments may be true to some extent, but the basic reason for Casy's self-sacrifice remains unspoken. Casy doesn't have time to explain, before he's hauled away in the police car, that he's found his way to show love for his fellow man. No one can now accuse Casy of being all talk and no action.

Uncle John is so moved by Casy's act of martyrdom that he blurts out a confession. He's been holding out $5 from the family coffers to get drunk when he got "to hurtin' inside." Pa and Ma understand John's need. They let him keep $2 for a binge. John gratefully goes off to drink away his sadness.

Connie goes off, too, but not to drink. He runs away from the family, never to return. California has let him down. His dream of owning a pretty house and getting a good job has been shattered by Hooverville. "If I'd of knowed it would be like this I wouldn' of came," he says to his wife. Even Rose of Sharon, who frets and whines through most of the book, has a reservoir of strength to help her endure. To Connie, she says, "You ain't givin' it up!" But Connie does give up and sneaks away alone. Pa, not one to mince words, has the final say on Connie: "Didn' have no guts . . . all the time a-sayin' what he's a-gonna do. Never doin' nothin'."

Leaving Hooverville just a step ahead of the flames, the Joads' truck carries two fewer passengers than when it arrived. Of the eight people left in the clan, Ma ought to be the most disheartened. After all, she's been trying the hardest to maintain her family. But oddly, it is she who bolsters the others.

When a mob of armed toughs on the road stops the truck, Tom almost explodes in fury. Ma holds him back. Later, Tom laments, ''They're a-tryin' to make us cringe an' crawl like a whipped bitch. They tryin' to break us.'' Ma's response is a simple, but eloquent, statement of encouragement. You might even call it a pledge of faith in the people. ''Why, Tom—,'' she says, us people will go on livin' when all them people is gone. Why, Tom, we're the people that live. They ain't gonna wipe us out. Why, we're the people—we go on.''

NOTE: How can Ma keep this promise alive in spite of terrifying odds? How heavy must her burdens be before she breaks? Is it really possible to endure any hardship and still go on? These are questions that will surely be answered in the remainder of *The Grapes of Wrath*.

CHAPTER 21

Can you see the thin line between hunger and anger? Steinbeck tries to show it to us in this short interchapter.

Hunger changes you. You'll do anything to get food. And when people who do have food keep it from you, you're bound to resent it. And when you are hungry and you see money that could go to wages go instead to gas, guns, agents, spies, and a whole range of hostile acts to keep you down, how can you help growing more resentful? And when the resentment is strong enough, you can't tell it from anger.

And soon the anger ''ferments.'' Like wine, it becomes potent.

And the title *The Grapes of Wrath* begins to make more sense.

CHAPTER 22

During their brief stay in Hooverville, the Joads heard about a government-run camp at Weedpatch. Life in Weedpatch is reported to be humane, clean, and safe. Why, then, don't all the migrants rush to Weedpatch? Because while the camp offers all the amenities, jobs within driving distance of the camp are scarce.

Nevertheless, the Joads decide to take their chances. They drive to the camp and for the first time in California, hear a friendly word, find a comfortable campsite, and get cleaned up. At every turn, they find pleasant surprises: hot and cold running water, toilets, showers, even a committee of residents to keep order and run the camp. Every Saturday night there's a dance. And best of all, no deputies or other belligerent officials are allowed inside camp gates. In all respects, Weedpatch is a refuge. "Oh! Praise God," says Ma.

Tom is up first the next morning. Gracious neighbors, the Wallaces, feed him breakfast and invite him to come along on a pipe-laying job they have on a farm a mile away. What phenomenal luck! He accepts, of course, but bad news greets him and the Wallaces when they get to Mr. Thomas' farm.

Thomas tells them that he can't pay 30 cents an hour anymore. It's 25 cents, take it or leave it. The Bank of the West, through the local Farmers' Association, has forced Thomas to cut his wage. The higher wage, he's been told, causes unrest among other workers in the valley. If Thomas defies the bank, he won't get his usual crop loan next year.

Because the Association has pushed him around, Thomas feels free to reveal plans for a raid on the government camp on Saturday night. The Association hates the camp because people feel content there. When the folks go back to squatters' camps, "they'll be hard to handle," Thomas explains. Also, without a legitimate reason, such as a shooting or a riot to break up, deputies can't get into the camp. During the dance on Saturday, however, "there's going to be a fight," Thomas warns, "and there's going to be deputies ready to go in."

Since Thomas is so clearly an ally, Tom and the Wallaces agree to his offer and go to work. The other Joads aren't as lucky as Tom. They fail to locate jobs during their daylong quest for work.

Back at the government camp, Ma and the children spend the first day learning to be civilized again. Ruthie and Winfield have the most to learn. Can you imagine what happens to 12- and 13-year-olds leading this kind of wayward life? Lately they've seen almost nothing but meanness and violence and death. How can they be expected to act like sweet, lovable kids?

In fact, they don't. They argue and fight and call each other names. In the camp bathroom Winfield flushes a toilet. Convinced that he broke it, Ruthie delights in telling on her frightened brother. Perhaps their behavior doesn't differ greatly from any typical brother and sister, but Ruthie in particular antagonizes almost everybody. For example, she barges into the middle of a children's game of croquet, shouting, "I wanta play now." The children troop silently off the court. Seeing that no one will play with her, Ruthie realizes her mistake. She runs back to the tent to weep alone. In time, she'll learn to act decently, but as for many people, it won't be easy.

When the camp manager pays a call on the Joads, Ma is distrustful at first. She has every right to be. When has any kind of authority treated her respectfully? But the manager calls her "Mrs. Joad," and praises her coffee. He also informs her that the camp's Ladies' Committee will soon visit her. Ma scurries around tidying herself and the tent. Suddenly, her dream of a better life has been rekindled. "Why, I feel like people again," she sighs.

The ladies of the camp greet Ma warmly. They take her around, proud to show off the laundry, toilet, and shower room. The camp works, they tell her, because people cooperate. No one should go hungry in the camp. If you're in need, you'll get credit at the Weedpatch store. If you can't pay your rent, you can work for the camp. Your obligation is to be clean, quiet, and obey the rules. Violators are expelled from the camp.

Just when Ma begins to enjoy her new surroundings a little, she has a row with a certain Mrs. Sandry, who has come to visit Rose of Sharon. Since Connie abandoned her, Rose of Sharon has been sickly and lethargic. Mrs. Sandry, a poor, deranged woman crazed by fear of the devil, warns Rose of Sharon: "You be good. If you got sin on you—you better watch out for that there baby." Sin, to Mrs. Sandry, is "clutch-an'-hug dancin'," the kind they do every Saturday night at the camp. And "play-actin'," too, when folks go "struttin' an' paradin' an' speakin'" like they're somebody they ain't." Since Rose of Sharon has done both, she grows pale with fear over losing her baby.

Ma comes to the rescue. Remember how Ma threw the Jehovite woman out of the tent? She does the same to Mrs. Sandry, not only to protect her terrified daughter, but because she rejects Mrs. Sandry's "wailin' an' moanin' " brand of religion. Picking up a stick of wood, she says, "Git! Don't you never come back. I seen your kind before." The woman leaves, but she has left her mark on Rose of Sharon. Until her baby is born, Rose of Sharon will brood over what Mrs. Sandry called the "innocent child a-burnin' in that there girl's belly."

CHAPTER 23

Even in the worst times, people need a little fun. You know what happens when you work all the time and never play. It's almost an instinct to seek out amusement of some kind in the midst of turmoil. In this interchapter, we're told how the migrants amused themselves on the road and in the camps.

They told jokes and stories—stories of home and stories of fighting Indians and what happened in the army.

Some evenings, instead of eating dinner with their 20 cents, they'd go to a movie in town and come back later and tell the folks all about it.

Some drank to escape their sorrows.

And some played music. There's nothing like the harmonica, fiddle, and guitar to bring people together, get them to tap their feet, whistle, and dance.

Religion was a form of amusement, too. Talking to God lifted the spirits. A good preacher helped the time pass very nicely.

Steinbeck says, "The migrant people looked humbly for pleasures on the roads."

CHAPTER 24

Getting ready for the Saturday night dance, the camp hums with activity. The dance is a big event. For a few hours each week, migrants from the government camp and from the squatters' camps come together, shed their worries, and have a good time.

This night is different, of course. The camp committee has been tipped off that there's going to be trouble, but they have a plan to deal with it. Guards have been posted at the gate and around the camp's perimeter. Suspicious-looking characters will be carefully watched. At the first sign of an argument, 20 strong young men will converge on the instigators and sweep them right out of the place.

The crowd gathers, the music and dancing start. The young men and girls whoop it up. Ma Joad and Rose of Sharon have come to see the dancing. The older men, like Pa, separate from the throng and spend the evening in conversation. As you might expect, they talk of jobs, of low wages, and problems of feeding their families. They exchange news about such things as a working man being arrested for "vagrancy" because the cop didn't like him, and bosses replacing "two-bit" men with 20-cents-an-hour men on the job.

When Pa intimates that he'd work for 20 cents rather than not work at all, a man called Black Hat lashes out: "You'll do that. An' I'm a two-bit man. You'll take my job for twenty cents. An' then I'll git hungry an' I'll take my job back for fifteen."

"Well, what the hell can I do?" asks Pa. "I can't starve so's you can get two bits."

Doesn't this brief exchange define the questions that every migrant has to ask himself: Do I work for less than the going rate and put a fellow-migrant out of a job? Or do I let my family go hungry?

Later in the evening, Black Hat offers a suggestion that will make such impossible-to-answer questions irrelevant. Unions! If the workers form unions, they can get what they want. To illustrate his point, he tells about workers in rubber plants in Akron, Ohio. Townspeople were yelling "Red" and getting ready to run the union right out of Akron. The workers, how-

ever—all 5000 of them—marched through town with
rifles, and as Black Hat tells it, "they ain't been no
trouble sence then."

Black Hat's story moves his listeners, but they don't
know if poor and hungry migrant farm workers in
central California could ever form themselves into a
union.

Halfway through the evening's dance, though, we
see what strong men working together can do. A
guard reports two carloads of men with guns waiting
in the dark outside the camp. Jule, a camp guard at
the gate, spots three intruders, young migrant men
hired to stir up trouble. One starts to pick a fight over
a girl. The alerted squad grabs all three and hurries
them into the darkness. Under orders not to harm the
men, although they have every right to do so, the
squad releases them at the edge of the camp.

Meanwhile, deputies ride up to the gate and
demand to be admitted.

"Got a warrant?" the gatekeeper asks.

"We don't need a warrant if there's a riot."

"We got no riots here." Indeed, the only sound the
deputies hear in the camp is the foot-stomping beat of
good country music.

CHAPTER 25

Anger leaps from the pages of this interchapter.
You can almost feel the author's wrath.

Steinbeck starts slowly, describing for us in poetic
language beautiful springtime in California. The land
is bountiful, like Mother Earth. It brings forth big,
sweet, luscious fruit that makes the mouth water.

But lurking in this land of plenty there is a harsh reality—the economic principle of supply and demand. When farmers grow too much, food prices drop; when there's a shortage, prices rise.

At the time of our story, prices are so low that the farmers can't even afford to harvest their crops. So peaches are left to rot on the trees, grapes to wither on the vine. Oranges are burned, corn and potatoes bulldozed into the ground.

Debt creeps up on the little farmers and drives them out of business. Only the large farmers, the ones with canneries, can survive. Fruit and vegetables last for years vacuum-packed inside a can.

Now, here is the root of anger and shame: While food is being buried and burned, hundreds of thousands of malnourished, underfed people roam the countryside. What does a man with a starving child do when food is deliberately destroyed before his eyes? What can he feel but rage?

CHAPTER 26

Life in the government camp agrees with the Joads. But after a month of unemployment they are compelled to move on. They're out of money. They've resorted to eating fried dough at mealtime. Rose of Sharon's baby is due soon. If mother and child don't eat properly, their lives will be endangered.

A month or two ago, the men in the family would have decided that it was time to pack up and go. This time, Ma gives the word, "We'll go in the mornin'."

Pa's reaction to Ma's command is what you might expect from a man who's lost his authority. He's angry, downcast, and embarrassed. Uncharacteristically, Ma rubs Pa's wounds with salt, telling him that since he hasn't supported his family lately, he can't tell her or anybody else what to do.

After Pa walks away in disgust, Tom questions Ma's motives. Making Pa angry was meant to take his mind off his heavy heart, she claims. If a man can get mad, trouble hasn't defeated him yet. Pa is still "awright."

"I don' need to make you mad. I got to lean on you," Ma declares to Tom. "You won't give up."

Tom objects. He, too, would like to drown his sorrows in drink, like Uncle John, or prove his manhood by seducing girls, like Al.

"You can't, Tom," Ma responds. "They's some folks that's just theirself an' nothin' more. . . . Ever'thing you do is more'n you."

How are we to interpret Ma's puzzling words? Why has Ma appointed Tom to a special position in the family? How can Tom be "more'n" what he is?

Perhaps Tom deserves an annointed place. We've never seen him do anything frivolous or self-indulgent. He's awfully serious, ever mindful of the need to keep trying. Also, Ma may be telling Tom that she's getting too tired to continue carrying the family by herself. On the other hand, Ma may simply be advising Tom to be aware that his life has a purpose beyond itself. He has a mission. In other words, his life is destined to have meaning for others. Or as Ma says to Tom, "You're spoke for."

The Joads gather their belongings and prepare to leave. They say their goodbyes: Al to a girl to whom he's pledged undying love; Pa to the camp manager; Tom to his friends Jule and Will, who keep talking about the gains to be made if workers organize unions.

Almost at the last minute, Ma decides that Rose of
Sharon should have a Joad family heirloom, a pair of
gold earrings. But first, Rose of Sharon's ears must be
pierced. When it's done, we learn that mothers-to-be
need pierced ears to protect their babies. That, at least,
is what Ma tells Rose of Sharon to keep the girl's
spirits up.

Out on the highway again, the Joads' truck blows a
tire. While Al and Tom plug the nailhole, a car stops
and a well-dressed man tells them that they can find
work picking peaches at the Hooper Ranch, about forty miles north. The Joads drive directly there, calcu-
lating all the while how much money they will earn
and what food they'll buy. Family morale soars, as
you might expect after several lean weeks. Ma and Al
even dare to dream a little of better days ahead. Ma
aspires to own a house, and Al has thoughts of setting
out on his own and finding a job in a garage.

Outside the Hooper Ranch the road is blocked with
cars, policemen, and armed men. As the truck,
escorted by police motorcycles, passes through the
gate, Tom notices a line of angry men standing in the
roadside ditch. When he asks a man with a badge
what's going on, he's told it's none of his affair.

As quickly as possible the family rushes into the
orchard to pick peaches. Hurrying proves to be a mistake, because the first batch of peaches is rejected by
the checker. The fruit is bruised, he says. Peaches
must be handled gently; you can't throw them into
the box.

Working slowly and carefully, by midafternoon the
family has packed 20 boxes, enough for one dollar's
credit at the Hooper store. It's not much, but it's
enough to buy meat, potatoes, and coffee for the fam-

ily's first square meal in weeks. Ma uses up a dollar's credit quickly because prices are inflated at the ranch's grocery store. The fruit pickers could buy food more cheaply in town, but they can't afford the gasoline needed to drive there. They are stuck paying premium prices.

Under pressure from Ma, the store clerk gives Ma an extra ten cents' worth of sugar. But he puts his own dime in the till to cover the cost until the Joads can earn more credit. Ma is grateful and comments, "If you're in trouble or hurt or need—go to poor people. They're the only ones that'll help."

After dark, Tom, curious about the crowd at the ranch entrance earlier that day, decides to walk out there and look around. He's stopped by a guard who warns him to walk in another direction. You can be sure that Tom won't give up so easily. He doubles back, slides under the barbed-wire fence, and walks down the road. In a deep ravine he spots a tent, approaches it, and is greeted by none other than Jim Casy. Their reunion is warm and affectionate.

Tom asks about the ruckus at the gate, and Casy, who's been in the thick of it, tells all. The men are workers, lured to the Hooper Ranch to pick peaches for five cents a box. But when they got there, the boss told them no, we're paying two-and-a-half cents. Rather than work for those low wages, the men went on strike, and Casy himself is the strike's leader.

How does a man go from preacher to head striker? As Casy explains it to Tom, spending time behind bars helps. In jail with others Casy figured out something he never could have learned alone in the wilderness: One man in need, even if he shouts at the top of his lungs, can be ignored. But if everybody joins in the shouting, by God, they're heard, and the man's need gets satisfied. Or more concisely—in unity there is power.

Now there's a battle raging—the police versus the pickets. Abusive state troopers are trying to break the strike and drive the pickets away. If the strikers can stick together and hang on for a few more days, though, the fruit will begin to ripen. To get his peaches picked in time, the owner will then be forced to pay five cents a box. When Tom reveals that that's the pay he's earning, Casy is astonished. He realizes that the owner is using people like the Joads as weapons in the war against the strikers. As long as the Joads are willing to work, the strike cannot succeed. And when the strike is broken, Casy asserts, the rate of pay will be cut in half just like that!

"Tell the folks in there how it is, Tom," Casy says. "Tell 'em they're starvin' us and stabbin' theirself in the back."

If Tom took Casy's message back inside the ranch, would Ma, Pa, and the other Joads give up their jobs to help the strikers? Would other families abandon their work? Tom doesn't think so.

Suddenly, there are noises near the tent. Casy shuts off the lantern and goes outside. A bright flashlight beam catches him. Voices: "Stand where you are." "That's him."

Casy stares at the light. "Listen," he says, "you fellas don' know what you're doin'. You're helpin' to starve kids."

Those are Casy's last words. One of the intruders swings a heavy club at Casy, crushing his skull.

Tom grabs the club and attacks. Five blows and Casy's killer lies dead in the brush. Then Tom receives a stroke, a glancing blow to his face, but strong enough to break his nose and tear his mouth.

In pain, Tom stumbles back to the family's quarters, somehow eluding his pursuers. In one impulsive moment, Tom has made himself a hunted man. You can't blame him for exploding. He admired Casy too much to let his death go unavenged. But the word that's spread the next day says that the unknown killer started the fatal fight. Posses are scouring the countryside looking for a man with a bruised face, Pa reports, and "fellas talkin' up a lynchin'."

Tom's account of Casy's death moves Ma to comment, "I wisht Granma could a heard," for in his final breath Casy utters words that repeat almost to the letter what Christ said on the cross.

Removing Casy from the scene breaks the strike at Hooper Ranch. When the family picks peaches the next day, they work for two-and-a-half cents a box. A day's work nets a dollar and forty-six cents, enough to let the family eat mush, but not much more.

Tom proposes to leave the family. He's in too much danger if he stays. His presence puts the family in jeopardy, too. But Ma won't hear of it. She still needs Tom to lean on. Besides, the remaining Joads are gradually falling apart. Al, for example, wants to run away. He thinks, selfishly, that he'd do better on his own. Rose of Sharon grows more touchy as her time draws near. Uncle John, not a tower of strength to begin with, blames the family misfortune on his sinning.

Ma never seems to tire of figuring ways to keep the family intact. Now she devises a plan for Tom's escape. That night the family will pack up and leave Hooper Ranch with Tom tucked into a cave of mattresses on the back of the truck. If guards stop them, they'll say jobs await them down at Weedpatch.

The plan works. Out they drive with no destination in mind except someplace as far as possible from the area where police will be looking for Tom. They stick to back roads to avoid being seen. Late that night Tom, peering out from his shelter, spots a sign at the roadside, "Cotton Pickers Wanted." Tom proposes that the family stop for the night. In the morning they can claim jobs and move into one of the nearby railroad boxcars being used to house pickers. With the whole family working in the cotton fields, it won't be long before they'll eat properly again.

But what about Tom? He mustn't be seen until his face heals.

As usual, Tom is resourceful. He figures out a way to stay with the family and also stay out of trouble. He'll hide in the brush and sleep in a culvert concealed by willows. At night, Ma can bring him food.

Because chill winds signal the approach of the cold and rainy season, it's hard to imagine that this arrangement can last very long. But for the moment, there's none better.

CHAPTER 27

Picking cotton is tiring work. Bent over all day, dragging a sack from row to row, pulling the bolls off the plant, and carrying in the full sacks to be weighed tries even the sturdiest back muscles.

Basically, it's clean work, even though white fluff clings to your clothes, gets stuck in your whiskers, and stuffs your nose.

Watch out you don't get cheated. You're paid by the pound, and the scales may be rigged. But you can always throw a few rocks into your sack to make it heavier.

Fields are stripped of cotton in a hurry when hundreds of pickers, desperate for a few dollars, sweep across them. The money is good, but the work doesn't last long.

According to this interchapter, that's the whole cotton-picking story.

CHAPTER 28

Being in the right place at the right time often makes a difference in people's lives. The Joads, by a stroke of good luck—which they probably deserve by now—arrive in the cotton country of California just when the harvest begins. They are assured of many weeks' work. And they move into one end of a spacious railroad boxcar.

For days they eat right and have money left over for a few new clothes. Tom is safely concealed in nearby willows. Uncle John's thoughts turn away from his troubles and toward whiskey again, but he resists the urge to drink himself into a stupor. Rose of Sharon, growing ever rounder, has all the milk she can drink.

Al Joad finds a girl who's even closer than next door. She's Aggie Wainwright, who lives with her family at the other end of the boxcar. Al and Aggie fall for each other quickly. Mrs. Wainwright, worried that Al will soon go off leaving Aggie pregnant, pleads with Ma Joad to keep a tight rein on Al. Al's wanderlust never becomes an issue, though, because Al and Aggie announce their intention to marry. If the Joads leave when the cotton's finished, they'll go without Al.

Good fortune for the Joads, as we've seen before, lives a short life. One day, Ruthie gets embroiled in an argument over a box of Cracker Jack with some other children. She threatens to get her big brother, who has killed two men and is now in hiding, to beat them up.

To some, Ruthie's threat may sound like a child's bragging, not to be taken seriously. But someone else might start to poke around, looking for signs of a killer-in-hiding. There's no doubt now that Tom must leave.

Ma goes to Tom in the willows. Isn't there tragic irony in the situation? Ma, whose primary aim in life has been to keep the Joads together, delivers the word to the son she loves most that he must go his own way.

Since we have noticed that Tom has become more and more like Casy thoughout the book, his reaction to Ma's news can't be a total surprise. Like Casy, Tom has now spent time alone in the wilderness. He's thought about Casy's ramblings, especially how "a fella ain't no good alone." He's ready to take up the cause that Casy died for, to walk in Casy's shoes.

As he says to Ma, "I'll be all aroun' in the dark, I'll be ever'where—wherever you look. Wherever they's a fight so hungry people can eat, I'll be there. Wherever they's a cop beatin' up a guy, I'll be there. . . . I'll be in the way guys yell when they're mad an'—I'll be in the way kids laugh when they're hungry an' they know supper's ready. An' when our folks eat the stuff they raise an' live in the houses they build—why I'll be there. See?" Although he admits to sounding much like Casy, Tom is too strong an individual to be a carbon copy of his mentor. We can be sure that Tom will carry on his fight for the people in his own way.

If you've puzzled over Casy's belief that no one has a soul of his own, but that everybody's got a piece of a great big soul, you're not alone. Tom has worked at it, too. And finally, he's come up with a sensible explanation: Casy went into the wilderness to find himself. What he found instead was an understanding that he could not isolate himself from others if his life were to have meaning. In other words, his piece of soul was no good unless it was with the rest and was whole. Casy's—and now Tom's—realization drove him to spend his life being with other people and crusading to bring them together.

Tom has thought deeply about Casy. Ma's response, that Casy "was a good man," suggests his philosophy is all beyond her. "I don' un'erstan'," Ma says. "I don' really know."

Perhaps she doesn't grasp ideas in Tom and Casy's terms, but she certainly does in her own.

In the end, Ma, Tom, and Casy are three of a kind. All give generously of themselves, but each in his or her own way. They embody the novel's main theme and carry Steinbeck's message to his readers.

Soon after Tom takes his leave, the weather changes. Serious storm clouds move in and a damp cold settles on the land. Trying to beat the rain because wet cotton can't be picked, a local cotton farmer puts out a call for as many workers as he can find. The whole family joins in, including Rose of Sharon. In her condition, she shouldn't be out in the fields, but she insists on going. By midday the job is done, but not before brisk winds and rain chill the workers to their bones.

Wet and cold, the Joads retreat to their boxcar and huddle around the wood stove. Rose of Sharon, weak to begin with, has developed a high fever. As the chapter ends, the rain beats steadily on the roof.

CHAPTER 29

We've come to the last interchapter in the novel. Remember the first one—the coming of the drought? In this chapter we see the gradual inundation of the land. Day after day the rains pour down. The fields turn into lakes. Mud is everywhere. Dampness seeps into your clothes, your tent, into your very pores. It seems as though you'll never be dry again.

As the water rises, migrants flee to the high ground. Some try to build dikes to hold back the water, but the current pushes too hard.

Cars, their wires shorted out, refuse to start. Shivering people with no means of escape crowd into barns. Sickness and disease spread. Babies cry and the old die.

Then comes the worst news of all in this catalog of misery. There won't be any work for three months, till spring. How do you survive for *three* months?

You can't get relief, for you haven't lived in California for a year. You start to beg for food, even for leftovers and rotting garbage. As a last resort, you steal it.

No wonder the townspeople watch you. They're afraid you'll steal them blind. They hate to see you coming down the street. Soon, fear turns to anger. They call out the sheriff, the deputies, anyone who can smash an Okie with a billy club.

And meanwhile you starve.

Back in Oklahoma when the drought came, the women studied their menfolk hunkering in the dust. Would they break under the strain?

Now the women study their men again. Again, the men hold together. When fearful men gather into groups, fears dissolve and anger takes over. As long as men have the capacity to feel anger, they'll never break.

CHAPTER 30

Outside the Joads' boxcar the floodwater creeps higher and higher. Soon it will spill over the threshold.

Wainwright thinks it's time to get out, but Pa Joad has another idea. They ought to build a levee. Wainwright protests, "Be a lot a work, an' then she might come over anyways." Pa has no argument with that, and when he's just about to agree, the problem is resolved in another way altogether.

Rose of Sharon has gone into labor. That settles it; they've got to build the bank. Most of the neighbors' men grab shovels and start to dig. A fury of work overcomes them. Gradually, the embankment grows. The men are weary, but the fight against the ever-rising tide continues into the evening.

Inside the boxcar, another kind of struggle goes on. Rose of Sharon, with the help of Ma and Mrs. Wainwright, painfully tries to get her baby born.

Outside, the battle between water and mud has reached an impasse. Suddenly, a big cottonwood tree topples into the stream, tearing a breach in the bank. Water pours through and the men scatter to save themselves.

Almost at the same time, Rose of Sharon's baby emerges, a blue shriveled little mummy. "Never breathed," says Mrs. Wainwright. "Never was alive."

The surging water engulfs the Joads' truck. Al rushes to the rescue, but he's too late. It won't start. He's fixed and coddled the truck all the way from Oklahoma, but now it's dead. His job is finished. Later, when the family resolves to leave the flooded boxcar, Al remains behind with Aggie and the other Wainwrights.

For the third time since we've met them, the Joads face the problem of disposing of a dead member of the family. Uncle John at first refuses to bury the dead baby, but he changes his mind. He says, "I'll do it. Come on, give it to me." We see why he's suddenly so willing to do the job when he carries the baby's apple-crate coffin not to a burial plot but to a stream alongside the road. He sets the box into the current and says fiercely, "Go down an' tell 'em. Go down in the street an' rot an' tell 'em that way."

Who would have thought that Uncle John had it in him to do something like that? His action reminds us of the Biblical tale of the baby Moses. Rather than see her child grow up in bondage, Moses' mother sets the infant adrift in a basket. Moses "goes down" to Egypt, is picked up by Pharoah's daughter, and ultimately frees the people from slavery. What message is the dead Joad baby to deliver? We have to assume that Uncle John wants the world to know of the migrants' piteous condition.

With conditions in the boxcar as dismal as can be, Ma announces, "We're a-gettin' outa here, gettin' to higher groun'." The six remaining Joads march up the highway and find a dry refuge in a hillside barn. Off in a dim corner of the barn lay a weak and starving man. The man's little boy explains that his father hasn't eaten in six days. Last night the boy stole bread, but the father couldn't keep it down. "He's dyin', I tell you! He's starvin' to death. . . . Got to have soup or milk."

Ma glances at Rose of Sharon. The two women look deep into each other's eyes, speaking without words. Which of them thought of it first is hard to tell, but Rose of Sharon says, "Yes."

She asks everyone to leave her alone with the dying man. She bares her breast and lets him drink for his life.

As the book ends Rose of Sharon smiles mysteriously. Perhaps the story is meant to end enigmatically. Those of us who have accompanied the Joads on their long journey, however, may sense that Rose of

Sharon, too, has finally joined her mother, her brother Tom, and Jim Casy in recognizing what it means to be human.

A STEP BEYOND

Tests and Answers

TESTS

Test 1

1. The first member of the Joad family whom we meet is
   A. Ma, getting ready to serve dinner
   B. Tom, just released from state prison
   C. Grampa, drawing circles in the dirt

2. One of the famous examples of symbolism in the novel is the episode of the
   A. selling of the furniture
   B. swarming of the locusts
   C. turtle crossing the road

3. Jim Casy had given up preaching because
   A. he had been caught stealing church funds
   B. he had lost the calling
   C. his congregation had melted away

4. In her first and last meeting with Tom, Ma Joad
   A. stroked his face
   B. kissed and blessed him
   C. asked, "Tom, how is it gonna end?"

5. Grampa's death symbolically followed
   A. the meeting of the family council
   B. his removal from his home
   C. the breakdown of their truck

6. An ominous sign of what lay ahead for the _____
   Joads in California came
   A. from the Wilsons
   B. in Rose of Sharon's dream
   C. from the ragged man at the camp

7. When the family started to break up, the first _____
   to go was
   A. the oldest son, Noah
   B. sixteen-year-old Al
   C. Connie, Rose of Sharon's husband

8. Tom was saved from arrest when the blame _____
   for assaulting the deputy was accepted by
   A. Jim Casy
   B. Ivy Wilson
   C. Ezra Huston

9. Steinbeck's attempt at a Christ figure is _____
   personified by
   A. Tom Joad
   B. Pa Joad
   C. Jim Casy

10. The landowners tried to upset the _____
    government camp because they
    A. were afraid that the migrants would
       organize
    B. wanted to encourage a ''Turkey Shoot''
    C. wanted the migrants to return home

11. Is Tom, Casy, or Ma the hero of *The Grapes of Wrath?* Or
    can no one person be singled out as the hero of the
    novel? Discuss.

12. Analyze the reasons for the Joad family's disintegration,
    referring specifically to the departure of four family
    members.

13. Casy says near the beginning of the story that he loves people so much he's "fit to bust." Show how he puts that feeling into action in the course of the novel.

14. How does *The Grapes of Wrath* enlarge on the conventional idea of a family? Identify two different families in the novel and discuss their contribution to any of the novel's principal themes.

15. Ma should be considered a failure because she did not accomplish what she set out to do—namely, keep her family together. Discuss.

Test 2

1. When Tom leaves, he is committed to   _____
   A. carrying on the work Jim Casy started
   B. getting even with the cops who killed Casy
   C. "stop beatin' my brains to death"

2. The "blue shriveled little mummy" was   _____
   A. Muley Graves
   B. Rose of Sharon's baby
   C. the starving little Winfield

3. Steinbeck's vivid message of the need for   _____
   people to help each other is seen in the
       I. building of the dam
      II. stew given to the children
     III. breast feeding of the stranger
   A. I and II only
   B. I and III only
   C. I, II, and III

4. A principal feature of the book is the   _____
       I. growth of Tom Joad
      II. movement from personal concerns to concerns for humanity

III. plea for rotation of crops
A. I and II only
B. I and III only
C. I, II, and III

5. Ma Joad gets her husband angry in order to   _____
   A. draw a lesson for the family
   B. energize him
   C. keep his mind off their economic plight

6. The character who was filled with guilt over   _____
   the death of his young wife is
   A. Noah
   B. Uncle John
   C. Mr. Wainwright

7. Ma Joad's great strength was seen in the   _____
   episode of
   A. Granma's death
   B. the square dance at the government
      camp
   C. the job at Weedpatch

8. The line we associate with Jim Casy is   _____
   A. "All that lives is holy"
   B. "We make our church where our hearts
      are"
   C. "I'll pray for you if you pray for me"

9. In the midst of their travels, the Joads were   _____
   surprised to learn that
   A. President Roosevelt was coming to their
      Hooverville
   B. they were wanted by the police
   C. they were looked upon as bums

10. *The Grapes of Wrath* is known as   _____
    I. a religious allegory

    II. a sociological document

    III. a novel of social protest

A. I and II only

B. I and III only

C. II and III only

11. If you want to learn something about the union move-ment in America, *The Grapes of Wrath* is probably as good a book to read as any textbook on the subject. Would you go along with that statement? Explain.

12. Analyze in detail the personality of Tom Joad. Is he as mean as he often seems? What redeeming qualities does he have, if any?

13. If you were the librarian of an American embassy abroad would you want *The Grapes of Wrath* on your shelves for foreigners to read? Explain why or why not.

14. Do you agree with some readers of *The Grapes of Wrath* who, when asked what the book was about, replied, "It's about hatred"?

15. The social problem that gave *The Grapes of Wrath* its impact has disappeared since 1939. Do you think the novel nevertheless has some universal or enduring qualities that make it relevant to contemporary life?

ANSWERS

Test 1

1. B   **2.** C   **3.** B   **4.** A   **5.** B   **6.** C

7. A   **8.** A   **9.** C   **10.** A

    11.   You have plenty of options on this question because you can define a hero in several ways. Is a hero someone who lives according to a set of beliefs, maybe even dies for his principles? If so, then Casy would have to be your choice.

If you say a hero must be a tower of strength and protector of the weak, use Ma.

Tom qualifies if you think that his effort to change others as well as his willingness to change himself gives him heroic stature.

But if a hero must possess the quality normally associated with "heroism"—i.e., bulldog courage—all three would do. It takes courage to go on and on like Ma. Tom bravely defends Floyd and takes up Casy's cause in spite of the danger to himself. Casy sacrifices himself, first for Tom and then for the strikers.

12.　Crises sometimes bring people together. But not the Joads. Their crisis was too deep and went on too long to keep the group closely knit.

Dissolution starts almost immediately after the Joads get on the road. Death claims Grampa and then Granma. Breaking their ties to the land and to each other almost guarantees the old couple's demise. They can't be expected to adapt to the Joads' new way of life.

Lack of will sends Noah down the river, and Connie gives in to fear. Both lacked the backbone of the rest of the family.

Casy leaves for jail in order to save Tom. Later, Tom leaves to save himself. Neither really had a choice. Casy sacrificed himself because he needed to find purpose in life, as well as to demonstrate his love of people. Tom went away so he wouldn't be taken away.

Al's departure has nothing to do with courage or cowardice. He simply wanted to get married.

13.　What is love, anyway? Casy would probably say that you can't define it, but you certainly can demonstrate it. He shows his love for people by doing things for them. His expressions of love almost always involve some self-sacrifice. It could be a relatively minor deed, as when he allows

Granma to talk him into saying grace. Praying makes him feel like a hypocrite, but he'll do it for Granma.

Leading the strike at Hooper Ranch is an act of love, too. He ignores the perils of organizing workers because he knows that a successful strike will change the people's lives.

In a sense, kicking the kneeling deputy in the back of the neck was a loving act, too, since its purpose was to save Floyd from being shot. Finally, what else but love could have led Casy to let himself, instead of Tom, be arrested?

Near the beginning of the story, Casy claims to love mankind, but he doesn't know how to show it. Ma Joad teaches him, however. Think of what Casy says after he hears that Ma cradled Granma's body all through the nightlong ride across the desert.

14. The most obvious family in the novel is the Joads, all three generations of them, from Grampa to Winfield. The book tells the story of their flight from the Dust Bowl and their experiences in California. Their disintegration as a traditional family suggests what is happening to the whole society.

Then, you have the "Joads plus," consisting of the core family and others. Casy is adopted as a member. The Wilsons and Wainwrights become temporary partners. When families join with others, their chances of survival multiply. In that sense, the labor union is a type of family, too.

Ma Joad attains an even larger vision of "family." It includes "anybody." It is family unity and strength imparted to the whole human race, and is dramatically symbolized by Rose of Sharon's nursing of the dying stranger.

15. Failure is a slippery word. If all your efforts to achieve a goal come to absolutely nothing, is that failure? If you strive to reach a goal but end up with something different but equally worthy, is that failure? What if you end up with something better? You missed your goal, but did you fail? Answer such questions before you decide whether Ma Joad was a failure.

Another way to tackle this question is to ask whether Ma's dissolving family ever had a real chance to remain intact. Consider the roving of the migrants. Does instability breed more instability? Is there anything else that Ma could have done to keep the Joads together? Is so, perhaps she did fail. If she did all that could be done, perhaps you'd have to draw another conclusion.

Finally, what does Ma herself think about losing her immediate family? At the end of the book she talks about "anybody" being part of the family. Would someone who thinks she's failed with a few people turn around and enfold all of Mankind in her arms?

Test 2

1. B   2. B   3. C   4. A   5. B   6. B
7. A   8. A   9. C   10. C

11. Both the main narrative and the interchapters of *The Grapes of Wrath* refer to labor unions and to the issues we commonly think of when labor and management collide: the rights of strikers; strike-breaking; the public interest; negotiating agreements. The account of the Hooper Ranch strike in Chapter 26 may help you locate additional strike-related matters.

In the book's pages you also find allusions to such practices as blacklisting and planting "stools" (stool-pigeons) among the workers. See Floyd's conversation with Tom at the Hooverville camp (Chapter 20) and the men's discussion at the Saturday night dance (Chapter 24) for more details.

The narrative sections of the novel show the book's characters engaged for better or worse in union talk and activity. The interchapters (especially Chapter 14) identify the conditions that seeded America's union movement.

A word of caution: the employers' point of view is missing from the novel.

12. Since he is one of the main characters in a long and complex book, Tom is likely to have more than one side to his personality. Look for personality changes. Do his actions and interests change during the course of the novel? He acts one way with the truck driver who gives him a lift and quite another when he meets Casy. He's thoughtful around the campfire with Muley and Casy, but he's a man of action when the deputy is about to arrest Floyd.

Much of the time he insults and denounces people—the truck driver, the fat service-station attendant, the one-eyed junkyard man, even his brother Al. Why? Certainly not to condemn them. He hopes to arouse their anger as a way to release them from self-pity. Angry men don't give up; they fight.

To help his family Tom breaks parole. He's up first in the morning to look for work. He's quick to defend Floyd and even quicker to avenge Casy. Afterward, he's in danger, but stays with his family, anyway. When he is forced to leave, he follows Casy's lead and champions the cause of the brotherhood of Man.

13. Decide whether your job is to keep up the image of the U.S. or to help foreigners understand our country.

In some respects, the U.S. is belittled in the novel. A land of opportunity it isn't—not when people can't find work, or when they starve and die. Moreover, in scene after scene, authorities abuse migrants. A place that permits oppression cannot be "a land of the free."

Note the differences between the federal and the state governments. Oppression comes from *state* police, while a *federal* agency runs government camps where migrants live decently and with self-respect.

Another fact to consider is that *The Grapes of Wrath* describes conditions that have changed in the decades since the 1930s. Therefore, you'd probably have no reason to keep it off the shelf anymore.

Still another approach to consider is that the book may contain nothing worth hiding. In fact, the Joads could well represent what's good about America. They possess courage, determination, generosity, and ruggedness—all qualities that we like to think define the American spirit.

14.   The banks hate the sharecroppers, the Californians hate the migrants, the migrants hate their poverty. Readers sympathetic to Steinbeck's point of view may end up hating banks, police officers, landowners, shopkeepers, and anyone else who contributes to the migrants' plight. Surely, there's hatred in the novel. But simply because the novel contains examples of hatred, is it *about* hatred?

If so, it must be about other matters, too: love, courage, determination, socialism, prejudice, poverty, and much more.

The book makes frequent references, especially in Chapter 19, to a three-stage cycle of human emotions: 1. fear (Californians feared the migrants); 2. hatred (fear evolved into hatred); and 3. anger (the victims of hatred responded with anger). Reasonably, then, the book is about fear and anger as much as it is about hatred.

To claim that the book is solely about hatred may say more about the speaker than about the book.

15.   The Okies have disappeared. The U.S. has a welfare system to keep even the poorest people from starving. Guards no longer stand at state borders to keep undesirables out. Labor unions protect workers and have become an accepted institution in American society. *The Grapes of Wrath*, therefore, has become an historical curiosity. That's one point of view.

Here's another: *The Grapes of Wrath* is more than a story about the Joads and their problems. The Joads represent all victims of oppression and poverty. They exemplify endurance and the will to survive. Ma is a mythic figure, the earth mother—nourishing, strong, and protective of her flock. Jim Casy symbolizes the good and moral man; Tom, the man of action who comes to the rescue when the people are in need. These are memorable characters who stand for values held as dear today as they were in 1939.

Until prejudice, deprivation, anger, and frustration are wiped out, we'll need books like *The Grapes of Wrath* to inspire us and to help us maintain our faith in humanity.

Term Paper Ideas

Character Analyses

1. Ma Joad, Tom or Casy—which is the hero of *The Grapes of Wrath?*

2. In which ways is Jim Casy a Christ-figure?

3. How does Jim Casy turn his thought into action?

4. To what extent is Tom Joad a disciple of Jim Casy?

5. How does Tom Joad transform himself from an ex-convict to do-gooder?

6. In what ways do the roadside misfits in *The Grapes of Wrath* exemplify the qualities of defeat?

7. Is Ma Joad's revolt necessary?

8. Who are the stereotypes in *The Grapes of Wrath?*

9. How does Al Joad's coming of age take place in the book?

10. How does Rose of Sharon convert from a misfit to a madonna?

Studies of the Family

1. What are the roles of men, women, or children in the Joad family?

2. Does a generation gap exist in the Joad family?

3. How do the Joad family's values change in the course of the novel?

4. Which concepts of family do you find in *The Grapes of Wrath?*

Theme Explorations

1. What is Muley Graves' influence on the Joads?

2. What is the significance of Steinbeck's "I-We" statement?

3. Is the brotherhood of Man a hopeless quest in the novel?

4. Is the brotherhood of Man a realistic goal in the novel?

5. How does California turn out to be a land of broken promises?

6. What is the nature of the **battle** between machines and people in *The Grapes of Wrath?*

7. How do automation and human values conflict in *The Grapes of Wrath?*

8. In what sense are the Joads descendants of the American pioneers?

9. What happens to the Joads after Chapter 30?

Motifs and Symbols in *The Grapes of Wrath*

1. What is the symbolic value of the turtle (Chapter 3)?

2. In what ways may Ma Joad be deemed a symbol of America?

3. How do food, animals, houses, or caves derive symbolic meaning in *The Grapes of Wrath?*

4. What is the symbolic meaning of Grampa's rebellion?

5. How are the land and its people bound together?

6. How are Biblical allusions and imagery used in *The Grapes of Wrath?*

7. In what ways might the Joads serve as symbols of the American character?

Language and Structure

1. How do the interchapters function in *The Grapes of Wrath?*

2. What styles of writing does Steinbeck use in *The Grapes of Wrath?*

Points of View

1. Is *The Grapes of Wrath* a propaganda novel?

2. What role does government play in *The Grapes of Wrath?*

3. What is Steinbeck's economic philosophy in the novel?

4. Is *The Grapes of Wrath* a myth or does it show reality?

The Meanings of *The Grapes of Wrath*

1. What is the meaning of the book's title?

2. What is the American dream as portrayed in *The Grapes of Wrath?*

3. Is *The Grapes of Wrath* as relevant today as when it was written?

4. In what ways is *The Grapes of Wrath* a novel of social protest?

Further Reading

CRITICAL WORKS

On *The Grapes of Wrath* (general)

Beach, Joseph Warren. "John Steinbeck: Art and Propaganda." *American Fiction, 1920–1940*. New York: Macmillan, 1942, pp. 327–47. Reprinted in Tedlock and Wicker, pp. 250–65.

Covici, Pascal, Jr. "Work and the Timeliness of *The Grapes of Wrath.*" In Lisca, pp. 814–24.

Donohue, Agnes McNeill, ed. *A Casebook on* The Grapes of Wrath. New York: Thomas Y. Crowell, 1968.

French, Warren, ed. *A Companion to* The Grapes of Wrath. New York: Viking Press, 1963.

Levant, Howard. *The Novels of John Steinbeck: A Critical Study*. Columbia: University of Missouri Press, 1974, pp. 93–129.

Lisca, Peter. "Editor's Introduction: The Pattern of Criticism." The Grapes of Wrath: *Text and Criticism*. New York: Viking Press, 1972.

Tedlock, E. W., Jr., and C. V. Wicker, eds. *Steinbeck and His Critics: A Record of Twenty-five Years*. Albuquerque: University of New Mexico Press, 1957.

On symbolism in *The Grapes of Wrath*

Carlson, Eric W. "Symbolism in *The Grapes of Wrath.*" *College English*, 19 (January 1958): 172–75. Also in Lisca, pp. 748–56.

Fontenrose, Joseph. *John Steinbeck: An Introduction and Interpretation*. New York: Holt, Rinehart and Winston, 1967, pp. 67–83.

Perez, Betty. "House and Home: Thematic Symbols in *The Grapes of Wrath.*" In Lisca, pp. 840–53.

On the migrant workers in California

Anonymous. " 'I Wonder Where We Can Go Now'." *Fortune* (April 1939). Reprinted in Lisca, pp. 623–42.

Taylor, Frank G. "California's *Grapes of Wrath*." *Forum*, 102 (November 1939). Reprinted in Lisca, pp. 643–56.

On language in *The Grapes of Wrath*

Reed, John R. "*The Grapes of Wrath* and the Esthetics of Indigence." In Lisca, pp. 825–39.

Taylor, Walter Fuller. "*The Grapes of Wrath* Reconsidered." *Mississippi Quarterly*, 12 (Summer 1959): 136–44. Also in Lisca, pp. 757–68.

On John Steinbeck

McCarthy, Paul. *John Steinbeck*. New York: Frederick Ungar, 1980.

Steinbeck, Elaine, and Robert Wallsten, eds. *Steinbeck: A Life in Letters*. New York: Viking Press, 1975.

AUTHOR'S OTHER MAJOR WORKS

Cup of Gold, 1929
The Pastures of Heaven, 1932
The Red Pony, 1933
To a God Unknown, 1933
Tortilla Flat, 1935
In Dubious Battle, 1936
Of Mice and Men, 1937
The Long Valley, 1938
The Moon Is Down, 1942
Cannery Row, 1944
The Pearl, 1947
East of Eden, 1952
Sweet Thursday, 1954
The Winter of Our Discontent, 1961
Travels with Charley, 1962

Glossary of People and Places

Aggie Wainwright   Al Joad's fiancée. After a string of many conquests, Al finally chooses to marry Aggie. His engagement causes him to leave the Joad family.

Bakersfield   A city in the heart of California's central valley. Thousands of migrants settled in the surrounding area.

Black Hat   One of the residents at the government camp near Weedpatch. Pa Joad argues with him about whether workers should accept wages lower than the going rate.

Central Committee   The ruling group of residents at the government camp.

Floyd Knowles   An inhabitant of Hooverville who informs Tom Joad about employers' exploitation of workers. Floyd is about to be arrested when Tom trips the deputy.

Hooper Ranch   A peach-growing farm. To work there the Joads unwittingly pass though a picket line led by Jim Casy. Outside the ranch Casy is killed and Tom is wounded.

Hooverville   A term for the run-down villages of squatters' shacks in which migrant workers lived.

Huston   The chairman of the Central Committee in the government camp. He devises the plan to prevent trouble at the Saturday night dance.

Jehovite   Religious sect characterized by intense prayer meetings, wailing, moaning, and chanting. Granma Joad was a Jehovite; so was the woman who wanted to hold a meeting for her.

Jessie Bullitt   Chairman of the Ladies' Committee at the government camp. She takes pride in showing Ma the camp.

Jim Rawley   Manager of the government camp. He surprises Ma by treating her respectfully.

Jule   A resident of the government camp. A half-breed Indian, he helped subdue the intruders at the dance.

McAlester   The Oklahoma penitentiary where Tom Joad spent four years. After breaking parole by crossing the state line, Tom could be sent back.

Mojave   The California desert traversed by Route 66. Granma Joad died on the truck while the Joads were crossing it.

Needles   A town on the California state line. It's where state troopers "welcomed" the migrants to California.

Okies   A less-than-affectionate term for migrants. Basically, it means you're a son of a bitch and I hate your guts.

Purty Boy Floyd   A notorious killer of the 1930s. Ma knew his mother. Ma hopes that imprisonment didn't turn Tom bitter, as it did Pretty Boy.

Route 66   The main highway west out of the Dust Bowl to California. In the 30s it was called the Migrant Road.

Sallisaw   The town nearest the Joads' Oklahoma home.

Sam Browne   The name of a broad leather belt worn by troopers. To the migrants it became a symbol of oppression.

Sandry   The deranged, Jesus-loving woman who scares the daylights out of Rose of Sharon at the government camp. Mrs. Sandry makes the poor girl think her baby will burn in hell.

Thomas   The farmer who's forced to pay workers less than they're worth. He informs Tom and the Wallaces that local hoodlums intend to disrupt the dance on Saturday night.

Tulare County   Fruit-growing region in California. The Hooper Ranch is located there.

Turnbull   The man Tom Joad killed in a drunken brawl. Afterward Tom went to prison for four years.

Wainwright Family residing with the Joads in the same boxcar. Mrs. Wainwright assists Rose of Sharon in childbirth. Al Joad is engaged to Aggie Wainwright.

Wallace Name of father and son who invite Tom Joad to work with them on a pipe-laying job near the government camp.

Weedpatch Nearest town to the government camp.

Wilson Sairy and Ivy Wilson join the Joad entourage for part of the trip from Oklahoma. Grampa dies in the Wilsons' tent; Tom and Al repair the Wilsons' old Dodge.

The Critics

When *The Grapes of Wrath* was published in 1939, questions were raised about the accuracy of Steinbeck's portrayal of the migrants in California. What follows are two excerpts from articles written at the time.

The first appeared in *Fortune* magazine during the same month that *The Grapes of Wrath* was published.

> The migrants are familiar enough to anyone who has traveled much through California's interior. . . . They have become California's sorest social problem. More, they are one of the major social problems of the U.S. . . .
> Many of the migrants live in dirty roadside tourist camps, labor contractors' camps, or privately run tenting grounds, where the rents may be as high or higher but the equipment is more primitive. Some live in squatter camps. Conditions in these shelters are notoriously squalid, particularly in the Imperial Valley, which offers the absolute low for the entire state. . . .
> Many of the families camping along the irrigation ditches were using dishwater for drinking purposes as well as using the side of the ditch as a toilet. In February a child from one of these families was taken to the County Hospital with spinal meningitis. There had been no quarantine and the other members of the family were mixing with their neighbors. Children dressed in rags, their hands encrusted with dirt, complexions pasty white, their teeth quite rotted, were observed in these camps.
>> " 'I Wonder Where We Can Go Now',"
>> Fortune *(April 1939)*

The next excerpt was written by a newspaperman from San Francisco.

> The experiences of the Joad family, whose misfortunes in their trek from Oklahoma to California Steinbeck portrays so graphically, are not

typical of those of the real migrants I found in the
course of two reportorial tours of the agricultural
valleys. I made one inquiry during the winter of
1937–38, following the flood which Steinbeck
describes; I made another at the height of the harvest
this year.

Along three thousand miles of highways and
byways, I was unable to find a single counterpart of
the Joad family. Nor have I discovered one during
fifteen years of residence in the Santa Clara Valley
(the same valley where John Steinbeck now lives),
which is crowded each summer with transient
workers harvesting the fruit crops. The lot of the
"fruit tramp" is admittedly no bed of roses, but
neither is it the bitter fate described in *The Grapes of
Wrath*.

> —*Frank J. Taylor, "California's
> Grapes of Wrath," 1939*

Before *The Grapes of Wrath* was published, one of its edi-
tors suggested to Steinbeck that Rose of Sharon's offer of her
breast to the starving man occurs too abruptly. It needs leading up to. Here is part of Steinbeck's reply:

> . . . I'm sorry but I cannot change that ending. It
> is casual—there is no fruity climax, it is not more
> important than any other part of the book—if there
> is a symbol, it is a survival symbol not a love
> symbol, it must be an accident, it must be a stranger,
> and it must be quick. To build this stranger into the
> structure of the book would be to warp the whole
> meaning of the book. The fact that the Joads don't
> know him, don't care about him, have no ties to
> him—that is the emphasis.
>
> —*John Steinbeck, Letters (January 16,
> 1939)*

Many readers, including the author of the following,
have been offended by the novel.

To Steinbeck, the deadliest of the deadly sins is
simply being a typical American citizen—that is, a
member of the middle classes. Hatred of the middle

classes is in fact . . . one of the main "clues" to the understanding of his fiction. . . .

But surely it is disconcerting to find that the author hates you, the reader, with a powerful, compulsive hatred; that the tolerance he speaks of so smoothly is in fact never extended to *you*, and that just in having been born on the right side of the tracks you have committed the one unpardonable sin.

Now the mere amount and proportion of obscene language in *The Grapes of Wrath* are not, to be sure, especially high. Pungent Saxon monosyllables are much scarcer there than in the casual talk of schoolboys, where the same words are taken for granted and make little or no impression. But in *The Grapes of Wrath* these identical words *seem* more objectionable because the writer's imagination has so joined fact and idea, and image and word, as to startle the reader into aversion or even nausea.

> —*Walter Fuller Taylor,* The Grapes of Wrath *Reconsidered," 1959*

The moment in the novel that has provoked the most commentary is Rose of Sharon's encounter in the barn with the dying man.

Rose of Sharon's act, though dignified by various religious and mythic allusions, needs only its own power to demonstrate nobility. The transformation of her nature in a moment of crisis merely epitomizes the general movement of the novel from concerns of the flesh to concerns of the spirit.

> —*John R. Reed,* "The Grapes of Wrath *and the Ethics of Indigence,"* 1969